LOVE, SEX

AND

ASTROLOGY

LOVE, SEX AND ASTROLOGY

TERI KING

HarperPaperbacks
A Division of HarperCollinsPublishers

HarperPaperbacks *A Division of* HarperCollins*Publishers*
10 East 53rd Street, New York, N.Y. 10022

A trade paperback edition of this book was published in 1988 by HarperPerennial, a division of HarperCollins*Publishers.*

Cover illustration by Joan Perrin

First HarperPaperbacks printing: February 1994

Printed in the United States of America

HarperPaperbacks and colophon are trademarks of HarperCollins*Publishers*

10 9 8 7 6

CONTENTS

INTRODUCTION TO ASTROLOGY   ix

ARIES
(March 21st to April 20th)   1
Table of attractions   6
The partnerships   7
Are you a typical Arietian man?   19
Are you a typical Arietian woman?   21

TAURUS
(April 21st to May 21st)   23
Table of attractions   28
The partnerships   29
Are you a typical Taurean man?   41
Are you a typical Taurean woman?   42

GEMINI
(May 22nd to June 21st)   44
Table of attractions   49
The partnerships   50
Are you a typical Geminian man?   62
Are you a typical Geminian woman?   64

CANCER
(June 22nd to July 22nd)   66
Table of attractions   71
The partnerships   72
Are you a typical Cancerian man?   83
Are you a typical Cancerian woman?   84

LEO
(July 23rd to August 23rd)   87
Table of attractions   92
The partnerships   93
Are you a typical Leo man?   106
Are you a typical Leo woman?   108

VIRGO
(August 24th to September 23rd)   110
Table of attractions   115
The partnerships   116
Are you a typical Virgo man?   129
Are you a typical Virgo woman?   131

LIBRA
(September 24th to October 23rd)   133
Table of attractions   138
The partnerships   139
Are you a typical Libran man?   153
Are you a typical Libran woman?   154

SCORPIO
(October 24th to November 22nd)   156
Table of attractions   161
The partnerships   162
Are you a typical Scorpio man?   175
Are you a typical Scorpio woman?   176

SAGITTARIUS
(November 23rd to December 21st)   179
Table of attractions   184
The partnerships   185

Are you a typical Sagittarian man?   198
Are you a typical Sagittarian woman?   199

CAPRICORN
(December 22nd to January 20th)   201
Table of attractions   206
The partnerships   207
Are you a typical Capricorn man?   220
Are you a typical Capricorn woman?   222

AQUARIUS
(January 21st to February 19th)   224
Table of attractions   229
The partnerships   230
Are you a typical Aquarian man?   243
Are you a typical Aquarian woman?   244

PISCES
(February 20th to March 20th)   246
Table of attractions   251
The partnerships   252
Are you a typical Pisces man?   264
Are you a typical Pisces woman?   266

FERTILITY AND YOUR SIGN   268
CHILDREN AND ASTROLOGY   270
HOW TO GET IN FOR COFFEE *(A guide for men)*   281
WILL HE WANT MORE THAN COFFEE? *(A guide for women)* 286
ANSWERS TO QUESTIONNAIRES   291

INTRODUCTION

Astrology is a complex science which has of necessity been treated in a general way in the following pages. I should, however, like to discuss briefly the mechanics of the subject in the hope of correcting any misconceptions that the reader may start with.

The cynic will usually ask: "How can a forecast for any zodiac sign be accurate for everyone born under that sign?" The obvious answer is of course that all horoscopes must be general unless the astrologer is able to work from specific details about the hour, day and year of birth of the individual in question.

As an example, let us take a person born on 3rd April. Broadly speaking he or she is a subject of Aries, an Arietian, for the Sun occupies that section of the sky known as Aries between 21st March and 20th April. We must also, however, account for the position of the Moon, which enters a fresh sign approximately every forty-eight hours. It may have occupied Gemini on the day in question, and in this instance our subject would become an Arietian/Geminian. (Here it must be explained that the Sun rules will-power and feelings, and the Moon rules the subconscious, and so our particular case will have the will-power of an Arietian and the subconscious of a Geminian.)

Progressing further, we must consider the sign rising at the exact time of birth. This is an ever-changing process as it takes approximately two hours for each sign to pass over the horizon. It may be that Aries was ascending on the hour in question, in which case the image presented to the world—the personality—would again be Arietian, thus making our example an Arietian/Geminian/Arietian. This procedure is carried on through all nine planets, each depicting a feature of the subject's make-up: their position, the signs they occupy and the aspects formed from one another all play an important part. Should an astrologer calculate and interpret these movements, then we would have what is known as a birth chart. Due to the constant changes in the heavens, persons sharing a birth chart are very rare, but it obviously happens when two babies are born in the same place and at exactly the same time. In this event, as both children are endowed with identical gifts, environment will be the deciding factor dictating which characteristics are used constructively and which destructively.

If we return to our example we will notice that two of the three important characteristics are in Aries, and so our subject will be a typical Arietian. If, on the other hand, his Sun were to be in Aries with the Moon and Ascendant both in Scorpio, then he would display all of the traits associated with a true Scorpian, despite probable belief to the contrary.

Astrology can be used to assess many aspects of human life. The main purpose of this book is to assess the mating possibilities of people with others of their own or different astrological signs. There is a section for each sign of the zodiac which begins with a general character analysis of people born under that sign. This analysis distinguishes between the higher type—those people who use the characteristics associated with their sign constructively—and the lower type—those people in whom these characteristics are exaggerated or perverted.

Next in each section come two tables of attractions, one for men and one for women. These are designed as a quick guide to compatibility and apply not only to relationships between members of opposite sexes but also to friendships between members of the same sex, and to business associations between either sex.

In writing about the twelve mating possibilities for each sign (Aries woman with Aries man, Aries woman with Taurus man, and so on), I have treated each individual as a typical member of his or her sign. It is possible, however, that the reader may recognize himself in another section hitherto not entertained as his sign. To help you in this, I have included a questionnaire at the end of each section. Have a look at yours, answer it, and see which other signs—if any—you are connected with.

The sections of "Fertility and Astrology" and "Children and Astrology" touch on two subjects which can of course be very important to the success of a man-woman relationship, but the full implications are outside the scope of this book.

"How to get in for coffee" and "Will he want more than coffee?" are lighthearted but practical guides both for those with ulterior motives and for those who want to anticipate them.

Astrology should be used as a guide to character—its original and true purpose—and no better form of character analysis exists. It enables us to learn about ourselves and our friends, and once this information has been understood and digested it becomes easier for us to accept our limitations and weaknesses, leading inevitably to greater inner peace.

The reader may be amused by the contents of this book, but nonetheless there is much truth written between its pages.

THE BODY

Each sign rules a part of the body, that part being more vulnerable than normal for those born under the sign associated with it.

ARIES rules *the head*
TAURUS rules *the throat*
GEMINI rules *the lungs, neck and shoulders*
CANCER rules *the chest and stomach*
LEO rules *the heart*
VIRGO rules *the abdomen and intestines*
LIBRA rules *the kidneys and lumbar region*
SCORPIO rules *the genitals and bladder*
SAGITTARIUS rules *the hips and thighs*
CAPRICORN rules *the knees*
AQUARIUS rules *the calves and ankles*
PISCES rules *the feet*

ARIES

THE RAM

The Sign of the Warrior
or Pioneer

March 21st to April 20th

THE FIRST FIRE SIGN: *Energetic, enthusiastic, impulsive, positive, enterprising, lives in the mind*

RULER: *Mars*   GEM: *Amethyst, diamond*

COLOR: *Red*   METAL: *Iron*

Characteristics of the Higher Male

The planet Mars endows the true Arietian with much drive and an ability to lead and pioneer among men. In sympathy with new thought, he will forever chase progress or new ideas. This is the sign of the go-getter whose enthusiasm is so great that it will inspire others to come along with him. In this man enterprise, energy and ambition are often boundless, and, provided these characteristics are directed wisely, the Arietian can go far.

Recognizing the importance of a good front, he is particular about appearance and meticulous with dress. His wardrobe may be inadequate, but he will inevitably appear neat and fresh for his clothes are kept clean and well-pressed, so that on emerging in the morning his appearance and actions will give the impression of authority.

As a rule, the Arietian male will prefer work which can offer some opportunity for personal leadership, for he enjoys overcoming difficulties and may go out of his way to challenge opposition. This type is always hopeful, no matter where life may take him, and his happy knack of forgetting failure can aid his endurance in times of stress. Unfortunately, Aries also confers upon its subjects a strong impulsive streak, which will frequently land him in situations which could have been avoided with a little more thought.

Love and friendship fill a large place in his emotional life and the same impetuosity and ardor go into them; no male is warmer or more frank in showing affection. But these tendencies are apt to lead him into trouble, for many sorrows will follow rash engagements and imprudent marriages. Mr. Aries may spend the years before forty looking for himself and his path in life, and ideally a final commitment to love should be postponed until the middle years. Regretfully, however, his impulsive nature will rarely allow this, and he may go through several affairs or even marriages while in the

process of his search. If falling in love for him is dangerous, falling out of love can be even more dramatic, as
loyalty and tenacity are not among the virtues of this
sign, and the desire for a change in surroundings or
companionship is often too difficult to master. Separation and divorce are resorted to in circumstances which
would not be found unendurable by those born under
more adaptable or forbearing signs, and his "me-first"
attitude is not an asset in a relationship fighting for
survival. Only if he can learn to give and take will a
happy union be achieved. As a rule, this subject is attractive, but somewhat unapproachable or hard-to-
get, and advice from others will fall on deaf ears.
Many problems could be avoided if Mr. Aries would
only guard against being too ardent, passionate and
selfish.

Characteristics of the Higher Female

These characteristics are softened in the female, although she will still display all of the warmth and
vitality associated with this sign. She cannot abide half-
hearted work or want of enthusiasm in those around
her, and finds the ultra-scrupulous person who weighs
every word and deliberates over every decision a terri-
ble trial, a feeling that is usually made abundantly clear
to the individual in question. Scope is needed for her
energies, and larger opportunities are sought out which
will enable her to sway and lead her fellow creatures.
This is rarely fulfilled in the ordinary round of domestic
duties, and so Ms. Aries can frequently be found on

committees or running both a career and a marriage successfully.

Serenity is seldom appreciated at its true value by this type, and is still less seldom achieved, but because of her bright and lively personality she is a delight to meet socially. Other and very different types may excel in planning details or in organization, but without efficient assistance from the Arietian the most desirable projects make little progress and the best-laid schemes fall to the ground.

The Aries female is extremely active in love, and not so hampered in following desires as her male counterpart. Unfortunately, the proud appearance of such a woman can frequently attract the weaker male, which will almost certainly prove to be disastrous, for when given the opportunity this female can become domineering and overbearing, and will lose respect for the unfortunate man who has allowed this to happen. Above all else a strong masculine type is needed, but there are times when this appears to be most difficult, for here is a female stronger than the majority of the male race. When unsuccessful in her quest, she is likely to grow tense and frustrated. Aries rules the head, therefore headaches are common when under stress.

Characteristics of the Lower Type

He or she will suffer from an excess of the qualities associated with this sign, but hope and enthusiasm will be replaced by recklessness or fickleness. He is always engaged in some new project or idea which is rarely, if ever, taken through to any kind of conclusion. Rushing headlong into activities which require tact and thought will bring failure down upon him. Past mistakes, however, are not dwelt upon, resulting in the same situation arising again and again. Enterprises are abandoned whenever the going gets tough, this being his own way of solving problems; the fact that others are harmed by such action is of no account to him. Love is something of a disaster area: loyalty is an undeveloped part of his character and he jumps in and out of relationships sparing little thought for his partner. Occasionally he may attempt to form a lasting union, but with small success, for his inability to think first or to consider others will usually ensure failure and separation. When badly perverted or unbalanced a sadistic streak will come to the fore in his sex life.

Physical Characteristics

The typical Arietian's personality is intensely alive, the movements quick and impulsive. He is energetic, muscular and will normally have a thick head of coarse hair. In many cases the profile can take on the features of the ram, this being enhanced by a long, straight nose and a protruding mouth. Health-wise this is a magnificent type, though his excess vitality can be a danger and he needs to exercise self-control. He should try to develop some faith in those around and delegate some of his work, instead of wearing himself out by taking on too much.

ARIES MALE

	Sex	Love	Marriage	Business	Friends (opposite sex)	Friends (same sex)
ARIES	•			•	•	
TAURUS						
GEMINI	•				•	
CANCER						
LEO		•	•	•	•	•
VIRGO						
LIBRA	•				•	
SCORPIO						
SAGITTARIUS		•	•	•	•	•
CAPRICORN				•		
AQUARIUS						•
PISCES		•	•			•

ARIES FEMALE

	Sex	Love	Marriage	Business	Friends (opposite sex)	Friends (same sex)
ARIES	•			•	•	•
TAURUS						
GEMINI	•					
CANCER						
LEO		•	•	•	•	•
VIRGO						
LIBRA	•				•	
SCORPIO						
SAGITTARIUS		•	•	•		•
CAPRICORN						
AQUARIUS				•		
PISCES	•	•				•

ARIES MAN tends to have coarse, curly hair; a long, muscular body with slim hips and broad shoulders; high cheek-bones; a long, straight nose.

ARIES WOMAN tends to have a muscular build with a thick waistline; a strong face with straight eyebrows, a thin upper lip and highly colored cheeks; a short neck; small feet.

THE ARIES PARTNERSHIPS

Aries Woman with Aries Man

Mr. Aries may explode into Ms. Aries' life, for he generally enjoys sweeping women off their feet, not only at the beginning but throughout the relationship—which may not be overlong. If he falls in love he expresses it well, as he does (not always diplomatically) his grievances. If something about or around her irritates him, he will not hesitate to criticize, and Ms. Aries must either remove the object of offense or expect continuous argument—the trademark of an Arietian relationship.

He is intrigued by get-rich-quick projects, and may neglect the more practical financial side of life. But even at his arrogant best, he does not wish to fight her so much as his boss, his opponents and any of his competitors who are not within earshot.

It should be remembered that the above characteristics also apply to Ms. Aries, therefore they will never be bored and this relationship can be made to work. Unfortunately, in most cases the attraction is a wild, physical thing that burns itself out quickly. When two people are inclined to selfishness and impulsive behavior, which is often carried over into their sex life, the difficulty experienced in trying to stick to one partner can drive them apart and into someone else's bed. Pride would then make life together intolerable, as the all-consuming love would now be replaced by cold disgust.

Generally speaking, there is just not room for two Arietians in the same relationship.

Aries Woman with Taurus Man

Mr. Taurus is strong and set in his ways, whereas she instinctively wants to be involved in new happenings and ideas; he thinks logically and carefully, her thoughts are confused and rarely stable. She could feel frustrated and cramped by his conservative attitude, while he could be flustered by the new ideas forever thrown at him. Each possesses the need to be the boss, which can lead to a spectacular clash of wills.

Artistic pursuits are important to him, and he has a romantic streak in his make-up which may seem peculiar in one so practical. Even cookery is to him a work of art and one in which she is expected to excel. He will try to share these feelings with her, but her interests lie elsewhere and artistic subjects leave her cold.

He demands ALL, physically and emotionally. In fact, he will want more than she is capable of giving, and this will cause resentment to flare up on both sides. No matter how much is given, he will remain jealous and possessive.

Sexually, each possesses a keen appetite but Mr. Taurus places sex above many things she feels to be of greater importance and she will accuse him of placing his priorities in the wrong order. Mr. Taurus can't function properly unless his sensual side is fully catered for; she cannot begin to think of sex unless she is completely involved in the outside world and thus stimulated into action.

Not an ideal match.

Aries Woman with Gemini Man

In this union Ms. Aries is going to need to develop a keen sense of justice and patience, neither of which comes easily to her. Mr. Gemini can be exalted one moment and deep in depression the next, behavior which leaves her totally confused. He is eloquent, artistic and frequently superficial, his mind ceaselessly working and often appearing to be on two different subjects at once. She may be attracted by this goodlooking, sociable and amusing man, but her desire to dominate could bring out his rebellious tendencies; though at times this trait of hers might amuse him and he might even laugh it off, at others he could revolt, lose his temper and walk out, only returning if sure he will not be pushed that little bit too far.

This man needs fun and someone to stimulate him mentally. Routine in any form is death to him. Any attempt by her to look after him or make him see sense regarding financial matters or simply a good diet, will need to be done casually.

Sexually they seem compatible for most of the time but he has strange moods during which he expects to find novelty and surprise. He could be stimulated by a pornographic book or film or simply by the things she may say to him, for straightforward lovemaking can seem too much of a dreary task to him and one he can easily find an excuse for not doing. To avoid such a bad state of affairs she will need to provide some of the spice he is looking for, but as Ms. Aries' imagination is not so fertile as his she could repeat herself and find a bored man on her hands.

Aries Woman with Cancer Man

It could take her a long time to get through to Mr. Cancer as he is surrounded by a defensive shell in which he hides his sensitive feelings. Once this is accomplished, underneath she will find a man hyper-sensitive and easily hurt. It is natural for him to disguise anxieties and to try to appear tougher than in fact he is. He will also want to protect her, but Ms. Aries has no need of this and in her frustration she will tell him so. This could cause him to brood or sulk for days.

The Cancer man tenaciously holds on to his ideas, his dreams, books and music, and she may feel they are her rivals as they hold no interest for her. He is in for a hard time trying to stimulate this inartistic woman with such romantic pursuits.

Sexually, he needs to lead in a loving and protective way. He believes that his woman should remain a lady in or out of bed, and Ms. Aries' direct manner could not only offend but shock him, for it takes a long time for him to lose his inhibitions and he may never do so with such an impulsive woman. He may not say so, but he probably feels that sex is primarily for the creation of children. He loves children and will want a large family—yet one more reason for clashing with independent Ms. Aries.

Caution is advised when leaping into bed with Mr. Cancer: he takes his sex seriously.

Aries Woman with Leo Man

This could be an instantaneous, fiery attraction, full of passion, warmth and absorption in each other. But trouble could spring from Mr. Leo's need for continuous admiration and for being treated as king of their castle, because Ms. Aries is not naturally demonstrative. She will resent his love of flattery, especially if it comes from some attractive girl, but if her love is strong enough she may see how important this is to him and do her best to supply it herself. She will have to aim at being his greatest admirer, all-woman and all-women rolled into one for him, or just simply the girl he fell in love with. His own contribution will be the tactful way he can handle her restlessness and need for new mental stimulants. While occasionally arrogant and patronizing, he may rightly point out that these traits are part of her own personality.

Mr. Leo enjoys his sex and is adaptable, and when he decides to take the lead he will be most appreciative, being open-minded to the suggestions she will no doubt make.

This can be an excellent relationship with effort on both sides.

Aries Woman with Virgo Man

Mr. Virgo has much to offer to the right girl, although his modesty, devotion and chastity may not be valued by Ms. Aries. She is a woman of action where he is a thinker. Mutual hobbies and habits could make this union, but without such sharing life will be difficult for them if not downright impossible. A form of rebellion could develop where each will put down suggestions and ideas for improving their relationship voiced by the other. Only if this tendency is checked at the beginning can they stand a chance of surviving the clash of personalities.

When in bad health no other sign is better equipped for taking care of her, for many Virgos are attracted to the medical profession because they love to sacrifice themselves, and she should indulge him instead of growing impatient. Finances could, however, add to the tug-of-war as he is over-careful where she is open-handed.

Sexually Mr. Virgo could be too ready to please this female, always ready to listen to any ideas or suggestions on her part. She may feel that half of these ideas should come from him, and when they do not she could become bored and restless. It is unlikely that such a union will have a physical basis, and if she is a sexually aware woman she had better pass this man by.

Aries Woman with Libra Man

A preference for living life to the full plays a prominent part in Mr. Libra's personality. He is very attractive to the opposite sex and conscious of his personal magnetism, forever in love or playing at it, with one girl this week and another the week after. His declarations of love should never be taken seriously until a decent period of time has lapsed, although he is not a total playboy and tries hard to create peace and harmony. This may prove too much for the fighting Arietian who is greatly stimulated by argument. Her Libran man will be disgusted and may walk away from such discord.

Though he will not become involved in a rat-race or fight laziness or stupidity, his strong sense of justice can lead him into battle on behalf of weaker and more vulnerable beings. This Ms. Aries will disdain as a waste of time.

When under strain, however, Mr. Libra can be as vicious as the next man. All she can do is try to discover what it is that has upset him and try to avoid it in future. She should keep back any urge to tell him where he went wrong as he rarely acknowledges his mistakes —but then neither does she.

Sexually, he relies on romance and enjoys playing at love even when married. He looks to her for response in this; she must be prepared for involved preliminaries ranging from a romantic candlelit dinner to actually acting out their first meeting. The moment a relationship loses its glamour he's off; any illusions he may have about her should be left intact, so she will need to keep him happy with sexy nightdresses—cold cream and rollers will spell disaster. She will also need to be ready for his lovemaking at all times. These differences need to be digested when determined to have this man.

A shaky relationship.

Aries Woman with Scorpio Man

Ms. Aries is strong enough to ignore any attempt by Mr. Scorpio to take her over, but her ability to give way will be severely tested for she will be sorely tempted to do the opposite of his wishes just to be awkward. Of all partnerships, this is the most difficult in which to achieve harmony. One of the main problems could be the Scorpio jealousy, which is a deep-rooted part of this man's personality and cannot be changed. While love is expressed readily, often this can be the sole side of the Scorpio man's feelings to find release. Woe betide the female who fails this type; he has certain ideals which she is expected to live up to, and when disappointed he may quite easily push her out of his mind and focus all his attention onto his career. His domestic environment is of the utmost importance to him; it is the place where he can relax completely and cut off the rest of the world. Ms. Aries, on the other hand, could find herself feeling claustrophobic as she prefers to be involved and living life to its fullest extent.

This man is probably the most loyal under the Zodiac, and usually mates for life—but this match could be the exception. Sexually, his jealous nature results in an overdemanding attitude where total possession is expected. The more intensely he pursues, the more Ms. Aries will run, building up a vicious circle which cannot be broken. Under all circumstances he is highly sexed and passionate but not adaptable; this must be accepted without too much bloodymindedness on her part if this relationship is to even remotely succeed.

Aries Woman with Sagittarius Man

Both subjects share a love of the outdoors, of activity and doing things together, but she could have her doubts regarding Mr. Sagittarius' ability to make a success of any lengthy relationship. And he may consider that she is ideal as long as she can come to accept his ideas on the freedom of the individual, can conquer her jealousy and ignore his harmless flirtations.

As he matures this man may come to appreciate the advantages of the domestic environment, but this cannot be relied upon, and no matter how old he is he will never outgrow the urge to gamble with life or to switch jobs at a moment's notice. Happily, for the most part his risks pay off—he is the original lucky charm. But when one of his projects does collapse, she will find herself landed with the responsibility of supporting them both until he has recovered, paid his debts and lavished her with extravagant presents to make up for it. In time Ms. Aries could find herself living in dread of the next crazy inspiration, though he can surprise in a variety of nice ways too. At least her life will never be humdrum, if she can withstand so much chaos.

This is not a naturally faithful man, for he tends to feel completely at ease when involved in several affairs, apparently unaffected by guilt. He prides himself on being a regular Casanova in bed and will never frustrate her as that would be a blow to his masculine pride. This side of their relationship should be satisfying as well as surprising at times.

A good partnership.

Aries Woman with Capricorn Man

Ms. Aries has been known to suffer from practical moods from time to time, and while in this frame of mind she could be attracted to Mr. Capricorn. She may admire his ambitious ideas, and his love of independence coincides with her own. On his side, her warmth, vitality and strength of character could appeal quite strongly to him. In a close relationship, however, the time spent on his career can arouse uncharacteristic jealousy in her. Life, she feels, holds more than a constant involvement in work. Basically, this is a simple man and she may be too overwhelming for him. Also, where his common sense will tell him that risk is sheer stupidity, she will want to gamble and will not appreciate the pessimistic gloom with which he surrounds her enthusiasms. On occasions she can bring him out of his depressions, but this will not avert violent quarrels.

The physical act for him is usually accompanied by romantic overtures, a characteristic she would be wise

to cultivate and participate in, for it can aid her in keeping his interest and their lovemaking very much alive.
Although the Capricorn man is not usually highly
sexed, the experience will mean a great deal to him and
offense is taken quickly if he is rejected with flimsy excuses. The depression mentioned above is usually carried over into the sexual side of life, and she must resign
herself occasionally to nun-like virtues until he is ready
to participate once more.

In certain cases it may be possible for them to accept
the faults seen in one another, but in general the disadvantages outweigh the advantages in this union.

Aries Woman with Aquarius Man

This man is a reformer at heart and he will try to
change his office, his friends and the entire world, and
while he may not do any actual improving he can usually expound on what needs to be done. It is important
to him that Ms. Aries be a friend as well as a lover, and
she will need to get used to the unusual, eccentric and
weird people who can intrigue him, for she will normally prefer the company of more sophisticated, swinging and successful types. The latter can drive Mr.
Aquarius to distraction. He can unintentionally hurt
her when in one of his more detached moods, when he
becomes unresponsive and preoccupied. The Aquarian
male can easily become a jack-of-all-trades while
searching for a job which offers sufficient scope and
challenge, and while respecting his ideals she could

struggle with rebellious feelings inspired by a need for financial security.

Mr. Aquarius rarely overindulges in sex, he is far too engrossed in other things to partake in excesses. He makes love when he feels like it and she could come to regard him as a very selfish lover. Healthy sex-maniacs should steer clear: this is not the man for them.

An unwise partnership.

Aries Woman with Pisces Man

Mr. Pisces is a lovable character. His uncanny intuition and desire to become involved in her ideas or ideals can make him a good partner for her, but it could be a complex relationship. He will need her strength and comfort when disillusioned or weary, and just when she has adapted to his little-boy dependency he will suddenly assume the role of protective male. Ms. Aries is likely to be completely thrown on the days when he withdraws into his own secret world, shutting her off while in the process of working out some new problem. For the most part he is happy to let the decisions rest with her, until they interfere with his plans, when he will ignore them. While she may protect him and partake in many arguments on his behalf, he will be totally unaware of this, his strong perception apparently deserting him on these occasions. This man has no desire to change her, however, and she could eventually decide to revolve her life around his love.

Sexually the Piscean man is adaptable but sensitive— he cannot take criticism in this direction. His slight masochistic tendencies often come into play during the act of making love, when he will be stimulated by thinking that she may be unfaithful to him. This should never be mentioned later, as he will be horrified in the cold light of day. His tendency to go drinking with the boys can at times interfere with their sex life, and leave her feeling frustrated and ill-used, but generally bedtime is funtime with him.

A good union.

ARE YOU A TYPICAL ARIETIAN MAN?

Answer the questions below honestly and then turn to page 291 for the answer. Use either Yes, No or Sometimes.

1. Do you try to avoid thinking of your past?

2. Are you fussy about your clothes?

3. Do you think that greeting cards are a waste of money?

4. Do feminine moods baffle you?

5. Do you consciously try not to worry about your financial future?

6. Are orders hard for you to take?

7. Is it hard for you to delegate your work to others?

8. Do you consider yourself to be a good "ideas man"?

9. Are you possessive?

10. Does motor racing appeal to you?

11. When your woman wants to make love after a very exhausting day, do you refuse?

12. Do you often feel sadistic when making love?

13. Is it hard for you to express your thoughts when making love?

14. Do you believe that emotional men are weak men?

15. Do you get annoyed when other men stare at your woman?

16. Are the comforts of life important to you?

17. Do you enjoy the company of small children?

18. Is it hard for you to switch off business?

19. When your woman is on the phone and you don't know to whom she is speaking does it bother you?

20. Is it difficult for you to accept NO from a girl you really fancy?

Score three for every Yes, two for every Sometimes and one for every No, then add up your score and turn to page 291.

ARE YOU A TYPICAL ARIETIAN WOMAN?

Answer the questions below then turn to page 292 for the answer. Use Yes, No or Sometimes.

1. Do you like expensive clothes?

2. Would you feel frustrated with a boy-friend who refused to argue?

3. Do you seem to attract weak men?

4. Are you impressed by extravagant presents?

5. Are you nauseated by women who have to talk to every baby they pass?

6. Do you enjoy organizing others?

7. If six friends arrive around dinner-time, could you make a quick meal for them without getting flustered?

8. Do you believe that a wife can advance her husband's career?

9. If you really fancied your newest boy-friend and he was a bit slow in making advances, would you drag him off to bed?

10. Do you believe that sentiment belongs to the immature?

11. Do you call up men and ask them to take you out?

12. Are you interested in Women's Lib?

13. Do you feel inadequate or uncomfortable around small children?

14. Do you express your displeasure when physically frustrated?

15. Do you cherish old love mementoes?

16. For the majority of the time are you quickly aroused in a lengthy relationship?

17. Does the thought of a good steady job for security's sake depress you?

18. Is it difficult for you to express inner emotions?

19. Are you an aggressive lover?

20. Does the romantic approach amuse you?

Score three for every Yes, two for every Sometimes and one for every No, then add up your score and turn to page 292.

TAURUS

THE BULL

The Sign of the Builder or Producer

April 21st to May 21st

THE FIRST EARTH SIGN: *Stubborn, steadfast, systematic, kind-hearted, persevering, often musical*

RULER: *Venus*   **GEMS:** *Moss-agate, emerald*

COLORS: *Blue and Pink*   **METAL:** *Copper*

Characteristics of the Higher Male

Venus is the planet associated with Taurus. She inspires in her subjects a love of the arts, poetry, music and painting, and the true Taurean shows a keen interest in at least one of these. The basic characteristics of this type are stability of character and of purpose, a steadfast mind unshaken in adversity, and quiet persistence in the face of difficulties. Mr. Taurus will not be hustled or bullied into a false position and he excels in work requiring a true sense of proportion for he is able to appreciate the value of method, order and system. Usually he displays a constructive ability, especially in matters concerning the foundations and beginnings of enterprise. He works his best when inspired by the love of others or when spurred on by necessity for he has a deep horror of debt, and so he shows much care in the administration of his affairs.

Although obedience can come easily to this man, when constantly nagged or goaded he will make a stand and his occasional outburst of anger is sufficiently vehement to cause considerable consternation to those who have aroused him. His dreams rarely lose touch with reality and he generally knows not only where he stands but where others stand also, so he will see through the false claims and exaggerations of more excitable types.

The Taurean shows himself exceptionally capable of faithful and enduring affection. His loyalty can survive rebuff or neglect. Love, for him, begins early and goes on into late life. The Earth in him evokes a strong craving for the physical presence of his loved one and any pretext may be taken that will bring him into contact with the object of his affections; the onlooker may scorn, the adored one may grow restive, but his steady pursuit goes on until it ends in victory or defeat. If a rival should triumph, a certain amount of philosophy comes to the rescue and disappointment is accepted without too much bitterness, for Taureans are rarely hampered by pride though frequently by shyness and selfconsciousness. If the chase is successful, it is usually followed by a happy marriage. His chief fault is generally one of obstinacy for no one is more stubborn than a Taurean with his heels well and truly dug in.

Sexually, this male would be classified as over-active and in some cases as downright lustful. Mental stimulation is not a necessity with him for he is always ready to oblige at any given time, and, though inconsistent with the rest of the personality, underneath the earthy exterior there is a distinctly romantic streak. Providing Mr. Taurus' partner is able to keep his needs satisfied in bed and can cope with the demands of his insatiable stomach, then she will find her reward in a contented and happy man who can overlook many of her faults.

Characteristics of the Higher Female

The female Taurean will share many of the characteristics of the male half of the sign. Both are strongly attracted by two things; the opposite sex, and food, and each of these is over-indulged in on occasions.

Gardening is a hobby often associated with Taurus, it relaxes and allows the subject to escape problems for a while. This female makes an excellent wife, shining in homemaking, hostessing and mothering; children are welcomed and are never worn out by fussy attention, constant supervision or correction. Ms. Taurus does, however, seem to suffer from a deep-rooted fear of financial debt and one eye is continually kept on the search for her comforts and needs. Her sexual inclinations match those of Mr. Taurus.

Characteristics of the Lower Type

This character keeps his good points well out of sight and often by trying to save himself trouble he creates even more. Excess vitality is bottled-up instead of flowing out freely to help others, for he or she is essentially self-centered and quite incapable of seeing anyone else's point of view. The normally splendid Taurean persistence shows itself in obstinacy and pig-headedness.

Tranquility is distorted into laziness and sloth, and the solidity of his higher brother finds outlet here in a foolish dislike of change, for he is over-cautious and deliberate. Likewise, financial ability changes into a materialistic view of life and a female of this kind is capable of making a mercenary marriage. The desires of the perverted or unbalanced subject are purely self-centered and no thought is ever given to the partner's wants and needs. This man can leave behind him a string of frustrated women and never realize it. His idea of a wife-swapping party could be to put the unfortunate female to work in the kitchen, but then if she turns out to be a Taurean maybe they will enjoy themselves in their own way.

Physical Characteristics

The Taurean is well-proportioned, built to a generous scale, the lower type being prone to gross overweight.

The voice is musical, the mouth sensual with a protruding lower lip. A sense of humor is clear and although the joke may take some time in evolving, it is usually a genuine achievement even though it will be distinguished for its breadth rather than its depth. His natural vitality, always excessive, should be used constructively otherwise it may consume itself and develop into morbidity. Dangers to health are laziness and self-indulgence, to which may be added sensuality, gluttony and drunkenness.

Of games in early life football is likely to be a favorite, singing is also found to be a congenial exercise. Throat problems are very common in this sign, causing much irritation, and probably striking when the subject is run down.

TAURUS MALE

	Sex	Love	Marriage	Business	Friends (opposite sex)	Friends (same sex)
ARIES						
TAURUS	•					
GEMINI						•
CANCER		•	•	•	•	
LEO						
VIRGO	•	•	•	•	•	•
LIBRA	•					•
SCORPIO						
SAGITTARIUS	•			•	•	
CAPRICORN		•	•	•	•	
AQUARIUS						
PISCES	•				•	•

TAURUS FEMALE

	Sex	Love	Marriage	Business	Friends (opposite sex)	Friends (same sex)
ARIES						
TAURUS	•					
GEMINI					•	
CANCER		•	•	•	•	•
LEO						
VIRGO	•	•		•	•	•
LIBRA				•	•	•
SCORPIO	•					
SAGITTARIUS					•	•
CAPRICORN		•	•	•	•	
AQUARIUS						
PISCES	•					

TAURUS MAN tends to have a big frame, often over-weight; a square-shaped head with thick, fine hair (usually dark); dark eyes; a thick lower lip; a thick neck; sloping shoulders.

TAURUS WOMAN tends to have a large body with a good bust and overweight hips; well-marked eyebrows and a determined expression; a fleshy nose and sensual mouth; sloping shoulders.

THE TAURUS PARTNERSHIPS

Taurus Woman with Taurus Man

The male and female of this sign are so similar that life will either be full of trauma or full of boredom. Ms. Taurus tends to run the home like a well-oiled machine, something he will love and respect her for. A sensible approach to the financial side of life and her strong business instincts both meet with his approval. She is a splendid hostess and can cope with a large number of guests as efficiently as she would with a dinner for two, remaining cool and unflustered throughout. This is important as they have a shared interest in the culinary arts, and food and entertaining are often an over-emphasized part of their life together.

The need to express feelings is strong in both parties, and they will constantly strive to convey their emotions to each other. The source of trouble in this relationship could be the well-developed Taurean stubbornness and jealousy: cross-questioning on each other's movements could lead to violent quarrels. The physical appetites being strong in both, they could spend half their life together in the kitchen and the other half in the bedroom. Their sex life is important to them but relatively straightforward. Where you have a Taurean relationship you find two happy, jolly and overweight people whose lives revolve around each other. Due to the similarities in characteristics—both vices and virtues—this union is either excellent or a total disaster.

Taurus Woman with Gemini Man

When Ms. Taurus meets this subject she will be wise to keep cool for a while before becoming deeply involved with him, as it would be too easy for a wild infatuation to be mistaken for love. Although Mr. Gemini is full of charm, once the relationship really takes off she should be prepared to work at it. Artistic interests should be kept to herself as he will be totally unimpressed unless she is up to professional standard. The last thing he wants is the domestic type; involved in a hectic social life himself, he needs a woman who can share this with him. Ms. Taurus' flair for hostessing and easy way of mixing with people will suit him down to the ground. She may, however, try to curb his tendency to flirt on these occasions as the Taurean jealousy is never far away. She is unlikely to understand his deep need to communicate; he MUST converse, analyze and mix with people, and her attempts to possess him could threaten their relationship. He admires the time and care given to her appearance and the talent she displays for organization. At times he will see the strength in her character and seek refuge when the world seems black to him. This may add an extra knot to an otherwise loose tie.

His chameleon-like moods may plague their sex life and are totally incomprehensible to her. One day he is a mischievous little boy and the next animal and basic. And her predictable reactions could drive him into a more imaginative woman's bed. She should remember that variety is the spice of life to him, in or out of bed, and if he cannot get it from her he will go out hunting for it.

Not a good union.

Taurus Woman with Cancer Man

Mr. Cancer could make her feel that she is the most important thing in his life, for he longs to understand every facet of her character—though he expects her to feel the same way. The domestic impulses are strong in both personalities and much time and effort will go into their home. This man will never take her for granted, an attitude fully appreciated by Ms. Taurus, but he is a dreamer, tending to place her on a pedestal, always expecting to find generosity and unselfishness. Should her flaws become apparent he will feel let down and retire into his shell. Ms. Taurus is not the most tactful person in the world, and clumsy efforts to coax him out will only cause him to retreat further. Her maternal instinct is such that it can aid her in giving the sympathy he so desperately needs, and she is also able to give a well-aimed push when his aggression deserts him. Mr. Cancer will not mind this occasionally as long as she supports him with her love. With the right amount of support and backing from her, he can go far in his chosen career.

This is a relationship that improves with age and hard work, as these are two naturally very different personalities. His sex life is much affected by the events of the evening; if unpleasantness has taken place he will find it impossible to make love to her. Any tendency on her part to bully will only build up a wall of resentment between them.

This relationship can be a good one with much give.

Taurus Woman with Leo Man

Ms. Taurus may be unable to prevent herself from falling in love with this man, for he has many qualities that strongly attract her. His strength, warmth and generosity draw her to him, while he admires her sophistication and effortless financial ability. Mr. Leo can quite easily ignore those aspects of her personality which irritate him, and her gift of expression will provide all the praise and admiration he needs to hear.

Some days she may feel that he is too sure of her as well as being dogmatic, demanding and overwhelming, and her rebellious instincts may be aroused by feeling neglected. Mr. Leo is excellent at providing all the comforts of life, the material things that satisfy her need for financial security, but she may not feel that this compensates for the lack of emotional compatibility.

This lack of concern for her feelings is carried over

into their sex life, and he could discover that war has been declared on him in the bedroom for his behavior may provoke strike action in Ms. Taurus; this would cause much distress to this over-sexed male. To retain harmony he must try to keep the romantic side of their union very much alive.

This relationship generally begins as blind infatuation but rarely progresses much further.

Taurus Woman with Virgo Man

Both partners in this union have a strong practical side to their nature. They are logical, with a keen financial ability, and so disagreements over money matters will be rare. Ms. Taurus is fond of attention, and Mr. Virgo likes nothing better than to fuss over and look after the woman he loves. The home and children play an important role in both their lives. Though this may seem ideal, neither of course is perfect. When he works long and hard at his career or on a domestic chore she will claim that she could tackle the same thing in half the time and call him a fusspot. And the strong critical streak in his nature could cause tension as Ms. Taurus does not take kindly to her faults being paraded in front of her. In time she may learn that the most effective way of handling this is to ignore it. While Mr. Virgo observes a certain routine and lives by certain rules, the Taurean has similar instincts and she should find this quite acceptable. He is an inhibited man, but she could be just the girl to bring out the best in him.

The Virgo man is not over-active in bed, but with

Ms. Taurus he will be about as sexy as he is ever going to be, because she can break down inhibitions and cultivate the more basic instincts in him.

With patience, all the ingredients for a close relationship are here.

Taurus Woman with Libra Man

Both subjects in this instance strive to develop the higher mind and all aspects of the artistic world are embraced and indulged in, providing a good basis for a relationship. But in everyday life he can irritate her beyond endurance; one week he throws himself into his work, hardly noticing her existence, and then suddenly he lapses into complete laziness, during which time all decisions are put off. Ms. Taurus prefers to plan her life where Mr. Libra will not commit himself for more than an hour, and her attempts to pressure him into action could lead to violent abuse on both sides.

She needs a man with a steady job and a steady income to provide a secure background to her life. His attitude, on the other hand, is quite the reverse. He loathes routine of any description and will seek a job in which he can express himself.

Mr. Libra is an incorrigible flirt, using this in most cases to boost his ego and nothing more. The Taurean jealousy could find this hard to accept, and she will have to try to control herself. Usually, however, Mr. Libra can tolerate her outbursts. Before taking decisions affecting their relationship she had better be sure they are the right ones, for he will soon blame her when things go wrong.

Initially they may escape the personality problems in bed, as the sexual attraction is likely to be very strong. But sooner or later they will realize that they have to live with the outside world, and this will slowly undermine their sexual relationship. While things last, however, both will treat the intimate side of their life as they would a work of art, trying to achieve perfection by experimentation.

A short-lived partnership.

Taurus Woman with Scorpio Man

Mr. Scorpio places tremendous emphasis on loyal and faithful relationships, because to him the world at large appears too cruel, untrustworthy and unfriendly for him to be left on his own. Self-improvement is a driving force in him, he wants to be the best in everything he tackles. Ms. Taurus is unlikely to approve of this, but if she attempts to restrain him he will become sarcastic, jealous, possessive and even cruel at times. These characteristics are a part of her own make-up, so a considerable amount of drama can be expected. If their feelings for each other run deep they may survive all this friction, and may even enjoy the daily combat. If Ms. Taurus wants a life full of fire and chaos then this is her man.

Sexually, both may have set ideas and may be inclined to expect the other to give way, despite the fact that underneath both are very sensitive. Both tend to over-indulge in food and drink, which may have an adverse effect in bed.

A brittle relationship.

Taurus Woman with Sagittarius Man

As a friend, Mr. Sagittarius could be rather good for Ms. Taurus because he can teach her to broaden her interests and become more flexible. Until they fall in love—and then the trouble really begins. The Taurean harbors a loathing of change in emotional relationships where the Sagittarian finds it difficult to sustain affection for any length of time. He is a sportsman, always keen to chase adventure and get out of doors, and when this indoor girl refuses to go along with him he can soon find someone who will. Her natural domestic talents are hardly given a second thought; he notices her and not her ability to make him feel comfortable. Mr. Sagittarius may listen to and digest her criticisms, she may even change him a little, but she will NEVER tame him. If she really loves him she will have to try hard to accept his restless behavior, and his optimism could be good for her.

Sexually, she is expected to be fairly versatile, and this constant keeping up with him both in and out of bed may prove too much of a strain. Unlike other types, he will want to enact his fantasies, which will horrify such a conservative girl. The first time he seriously suggests that they participate in some of his more way-out ideas, he could kill her love instantaneously.

This could be a great friendship, but anything further is ill-advised.

Taurus Woman with Capricorn Man

Although Mr. Capricorn is sociable, he is proof of the adage "still waters run deep." He may not appear at first to be very ambitious or even intelligent, but these qualities come to the fore as their relationship develops, as does a strong dominating streak in him. His keen senses note any worries or fears she may have and he will want to share her interests and ideas. A natural empathy exists between them, enabling them to understand each other's feelings, depressions and sense of humor. Both need a stable, secure and loving home life. A certain inability to express himself well can confuse her, but she will learn in time that his actions, rather than pretty speeches, convey his feelings.

Life has a good chance of running smoothly in this union, for only one danger zone appears to exist. This will surface when she feels like doing something wildly extravagant, disturbing his cautious and wary nature. But their compatibility of emotion and character is more than sufficient as a basis on which to build a good relationship.

His sexual appetite varies considerably from day to day, and he tends to go to extremes, being either over-indulgent or abstemious. He is greatly affected by outside stresses. The Taurean female will need to sense his tension and discuss it, thereby easing his burden, and this she can cope with reasonably well.

Taurus Woman with Aquarius Man

Mr. Aquarius is unconventional, loathes formality and does not recognize superiors unless they have earned his respect. He will converse with anyone just as long as they have something intelligent to say. Security and the material things of life, so important to Ms. Taurus, are unimportant to him. He enjoys work for the sake of sharpening his intellect and learning power, and changes his job frequently to satisfy these needs. Emotional outbursts will get her nowhere with this character; he expects differences to be discussed coolly and honestly. Emotion to him merely impairs the judgment.

The Taurean jealousy is once again aroused, especially by the time he spends on sorting out his friends' problems and reforming the world in general. Unfortunately for her, she can expect no sympathy in this direction. The Aquarian unpunctuality and disdain for routine and discipline are all deeply ingrained and she will just have to try to accept them or live with him in spite of them.

Sex occupies a low place on his list of necessities, although the need is obviously recognized, and this attitude may cause her annoyance. She will object to the whole world and its problems sharing their bed, and she may become over-demanding in his eyes.

A relationship to be avoided whenever possible.

Taurus Woman with Pisces Man

At first the Pisces man seems casual, adaptable and willing to do her slightest bidding, but later she will discover that he wants one thing one minute and the opposite later. When she is trying to suggest practical ways of approaching some problem, he will come out with an outlandish idea which may often work out better in the long run than her common sense might have thought possible. She likes her friends and acquaintances to look up to her, he is indifferent to anyone's opinion but his own, yet at times he is totally dependent on her. When problems arise the Piscean man will rarely discuss anything sensibly, he is inclined to put his head in the sand and hope the difficulty will go away. When tension is too intense he will take himself off to a pleasanter environment. The local pub has great appeal for him and the Piscean male is notorious for drowning his sorrows in this way. He is totally incapable of making decisions, for he is constantly torn between two directions. Ms. Taurus must be prepared to accept this.

Sexually, he is very sensitive to all her desires and tries hard to keep her happy, but if he fails and she criticizes she will soon find an empty space next to her in bed.

This match can work well providing the female is honestly not looking for a constantly strong man.

Taurus Woman with Aries Man

Ms. Taurus will have to accept that this is not a man to be pushed around or pressurized in any way, for his strength of character matches her own. A mutual weakness is their inclination to selfishness, the ability to give and take being underdeveloped in both types. And while she laboriously takes on one task at a time and sees it through to the bitter end, Mr. Aries will start and drop many projects because his interest is too easily charmed away by some new challenge. His desire to move around can clash violently with her liking for familiar places and people.

Mr. Aries likes to think he can succeed in a relationship, however; this, coupled with her stubborn insistence on continuing an affair long after she has realized that it is failing, could keep them together.

Sexwise, she may accuse him of inhibitions, for he lives largely in the mind, but with patience she may be able to draw him out. Unfortunately, this is a delicate situation requiring much understanding, and she will probably handle it with her usual tact—in other words, like a bull in a china shop—causing him to retreat even further, leaving her with a silent world of sex or, worse still, no sex at all. The Taurean tendency to nag unmercifully could bring out the Arietian sadistic streak. This might result in physical fights or, at the worst, in a sadistic sexual relationship.

Not a wise union.

ARE YOU A TYPICAL TAUREAN MAN?

Answer honestly the questions below using Yes, No or Sometimes, then turn to page 293 for the answer.

1. Do you consider food to be one of life's great pleasures?

2. Is it hard to change your mind once it is made up?

3. Do you wrestle with a lazy streak in your personality?

4. Do you believe the romantic approach to sex pays off?

5. Are you hungry after making love?

6. When hung-up on a girl do you long for her physical presence?

7. Are you persistent when refused sexually?

8. Do you hurt others with cruel words?

9. Do you regularly over-indulge in sex?

10. Can you become deeply engrossed in some art form?

11. Do you work harder when in debt?

12. Is your home life all-important to you?

13. Does borrowing money worry you?

14. When a relationship begins to show disaster symptoms do you hang on and hope?

15. Do you prefer to watch sport rather than physically take part?

16. Do you prefer to be the one taking the lead when making love?

17. Does the idea of being in bed with three or more women appeal to you?

18. Have you a strong jealous streak?

19. Do you eventually want a family?

20. Will your wife have to excel in bed?

Score three for every Yes, two for every Sometimes and one for every No, then add up your score and turn to page 293.

ARE YOU A TYPICAL TAUREAN WOMAN?

Answer honestly the questions below, using Yes, No or Sometimes, then turn to page 294 for the answer.

1. Do you over-indulge in food when your sex or love life goes wrong?

2. Are you almost anybody's after good food, drink and a convincingly romantic line?

3. Does financial security worry you?

4. Do you have strong ideas on what you want from life?

5. Does gardening interest you?

6. Is it hard for you to play it cool?

7. Do you take matters into your own hands when a relationship is progressing too slowly for you?

8. Do you have a weight problem?

9. Are you jealous?

10. Can you be revengeful?

11. Despite your feelings do you end a relationship if you suspect he is about to?

12. Do you like to lead in sex?

13. Are you thrown when faced with unforeseen changes?

14. Is laziness a problem for you?

15. Do you enjoy playing hostess?

16. Can cookery be described as an art form?

17. In health are your powers of recovery good?

18. Do throat problems plague you?

19. Do you believe that sex should be confined to two people only?

20. Do you over-indulge in sex?

Score three for Yes, two for Sometimes and one for No, then add up your score and turn to page 294.

GEMINI

THE TWINS

The Sign of the Artist
or Inventor

May 22nd to June 21st

THE FIRST AIR SIGN: *Restless, versatile, clever, exuberant, expressive, artistic, talkative*

RULER: *Mercury* **GEMS:** *Beryl, aquamarine*

COLOR: *Yellow* **METAL:** *Quicksilver*

Characteristics of the Higher Male

As ruler of Gemini the planet Mercury instills in its subject a vivacity and a surplus of intellectual energy which will seek expression in a variety of ways. Longing for new interests and an impatience with routine can, in the case of the higher Geminian, lead to brilliant results in literature or in some artistic field, for the subject is happiest when in the process of expressing an essential part of himself in some activity. Once this has been achieved, he will rarely rest on his laurels but will begin the search for a new challenge. This is an interesting individual whose true function is to make life more interesting and beautiful for himself and for others, in an effort to stimulate and refresh their minds. Intellectual satisfaction is a driving force, and should a new problem arise that at first is not readily understood, he will struggle with himself until understanding is reached.

The male of this sign in particular craves for perfect expression and the desire to influence those around makes it impossible for him to suffer alone or in silence, he must make friends and when they misunderstand him, the suffering often amounts to martyrdom. Any kind of sympathy is welcome at this point. Exaltation accompanying achievement is generally followed by keen and critical inspection, for the Geminian male is the most introspective of men, ever circling around in the hopes that he may eventually come to know himself; an impossible task. Loved ones should refrain from interference for he is best left to follow his own erratic path.

The Geminian male needs a partner who can share his mental interests, one who is never tied to the home and who is willing to change her environment at a moment's notice. She will need to adapt to his interest in other people, including women, and she should try hard not to take his flirtations too seriously. He can be surprisingly down-to-earth where his interests are concerned, and may not hesitate to terminate a relationship that appears to threaten him in any way. Guidance should be given without nagging for although home ties can mean much, he is temperamentally unfit to put up with constant pressure and will leave if his partner becomes too overbearing.

In the Geminian male there is the contrast of mild affection and passionate romance, as a lover he is teasing and flirtatious but seldom serious. Even when deeply interested, a bigger challenge can soon charm him away, for his affections are ruled by his mind and so he is capable of calculated action at times.

Characteristics of the Higher Female

It is impossible to picture this female alone, she needs people about her, plus plenty of activity and movement, and she generally manages to find them. Men are drawn to her attractive and stimulating company for trying to hold her interest often proves to be an irresistible challenge. She has all the virtues and shortcomings of the male counterpart, slightly softened, and is popular, gay, amusing, poised and always on the lookout for something to discuss and criticize, but a tendency to gossip is strong leading to tense situations at times. In love she is similar to Mr. Gemini, appearing to be fickle and a sore trial to her admirers, but she is generally ready to hear the other point of view—provided the other party concerned is able to get a word in, for Gemini is the sign of the talker.

Sexually, both male and female enjoy the thrill of the chase and the mental stimulation this brings, probably more than the act itself. Their partners could have problems creating the necessary stimulation, but if well-matched this subject can be loyal and sincere.

Characteristics of the Lower Type

This male or female will drain those who come into contact with them, demanding sympathy, attention, consideration and time, believing this to be their right. The lower Geminian will take excessively in order to feed his ego and will consider anything that does not concern or affect him to be of no importance. The longing for joy and variety, as enjoyed by his higher companions, becomes in him restlessness and perpetual dissatisfaction. He will constantly demand novelty and excitement but will avoid uncongenial chores to obtain them. Routine work of any description is particularly resented and if this is forced upon him he will feel doomed and caged like an animal, for he genuinely considers himself to be above it. This individual needs to be in the center of things, where the spotlight falls, and thinks himself ill-used when compelled to take a back seat.

Gemini is a double-sided sign that shows itself in the split personality of the higher type and in the homosexual tendencies of the lower.

Physical Characteristics

A slender figure is normally associated with this sign, also agility of movement and small features. Eyes are often blue or grey, bright but not large, the complexion pale though easily tanned. Quick, unexpected movements and speech are typical and Geminians are mischievous, taking much delight in their ability to shock. Their nervous energy can carry them through most things but it deserts them when a task becomes irksome or dull. Nervous exhaustion frequently follows their tremendous outbursts of activity, and health needs to be treated in much the same way as a child's, with above all plenty of sleep, fresh air and a sensible diet. Once the Geminian recognizes this he or she will benefit immensely, but a degree of rebellion may be displayed against this advice due to immaturity, for this type may take longer than most to grow up and many never quite make it. Children sense the mischievous tendency and usually take to them, much to the surprise of the subject.

GEMINI MALE

	Sex	Love	Marriage	Business	Friends (opposite sex)	Friends (same sex)
ARIES	•					
TAURUS					•	•
GEMINI	•	•	•		•	
CANCER						
LEO	•	•	•	•	•	•
VIRGO				•	•	
LIBRA		•	•	•	•	•
SCORPIO						
SAGITTARIUS	•					•
CAPRICORN						
AQUARIUS		•	•	•	•	•
PISCES					•	

GEMINI FEMALE

	Sex	Love	Marriage	Business	Friends (opposite sex)	Friends (same sex)
ARIES	•				•	
TAURUS						
GEMINI	•	•	•		•	
CANCER					•	
LEO	•	•	•	•	•	•
VIRGO				•		
LIBRA	•	•	•		•	•
SCORPIO						
SAGITTARIUS	•				•	
CAPRICORN				•		
AQUARIUS		•	•	•		•
PISCES						

GEMINI MAN tends to have a slim, sometimes thin body with long, slender limbs; light, silky hair; an animated face with wide-apart eyes and a wide, expressive mouth.

GEMINI WOMAN tends to have a tall, slim body with a small bust; high cheekbones and a wide mouth; light, twinkling eyes; a pale skin which tans easily.

THE GEMINI PARTNERSHIPS

Gemini Woman with Gemini Man

Mr. Gemini may appear to be her ideal man. He seems to understand her need for partnership on a high level. He agrees with her ideas on individual growth, and in intellectual matters they are in accord. He is able to be her companion, lover and husband whenever necessary, but unfortunately he will also rely on her maternal instinct—which may not be well developed—to indulge his childlike moods. And as she too can be childlike, this may lead to arguments, but two Geminians should be able to quarrel without bitterness developing afterwards. Too much friction, however, could be dangerous and their love will have to be deep enough to provide a rein for their tempers.

Their relationship can be most satisfactory unless one of the partners is of the lower type—then, it takes a strong and down-to-earth personality to cope with the other's deception, irresponsibility and aptitude for twisting the truth.

Sexually they are very much in tune and able to

achieve great closeness because needs are shared and thus they have mutual understanding. An awareness of the desire for mental stimulation in one another means that they each fulfill their search for novelty, leading in many cases to participation in elaborate sex games.

Usually an excellent union, but one which can be disastrous if there is a lack of strength on either side.

Gemini Woman with Cancer Man

While in one of her quieter frames of mind, Ms. Gemini could be attracted to this man's stability, peaceful nature and domestic tendencies. She likes the way he responds to her sense of fun, and the ready compliments which fall at the slightest provocation. If things go well, he may follow her example of speedy action and she could learn to be less insensitive to the needs of others.

In their home, however, he is content to lock out the rest of the world. This is where trouble could walk in the door, for she is a sociable girl who does not take kindly to being held prisoner. If she can eventually learn to share in his pride for their home and put up with his hoarding instincts, their relationship will stand a better chance—if she cannot, their life will become unbearable. No matter how intelligent, this man's actions in life are always motivated by his feelings, but although he is easily pressured by problems he will not run away from them.

Sexually, he is aroused directly from the feelings of the moment, and these can go quite deep, whereas her desires come directly from the mind. This may create much confusion in bed. They may never want to make love at the same time, and certainly the same things cannot be expected to stimulate both of them. He may be totally involved in his love for her while she is having some erotic fantasy, and as both are easily put off frustration is inevitable.

A meaningful friendship, but an unwise marriage prospect.

Gemini Woman with Leo Man

Mr. Leo is a determined character with a firm will, and has every intention of getting his own way in life, but when in one of his more generous and warm-hearted moods these traits do not seem to be quite so unreasonable. Ms. Gemini has sufficient adaptability to let him influence her on occasions. Geminians have a tendency to probe, to find out exactly what makes a person tick, and when she tries this with Mr. Leo she will find that under the proud exterior he is sincere; when he becomes over-demanding, he is only thinking of what is best for both of them. He respects her desire for individual and social freedom, but in return will demand constant praise and admiration. In company, she may resent his ability to attract the limelight, and may feel overshadowed.

The Leo man finds Ms. Gemini's changeable nature beyond his comprehension, while she can find no good reason for his phases of utter laziness. But he can forgive and forget her occasional neurotic outbursts, and she may come to understand that he will shake off his laziness in his own good time. Adaptability is the key-note of this relationship.

Sexually, again her variable desires baffle him, but he loves whole-heartedly, warmly and deeply, and this may be enough to break down any mental barriers she may have built by harboring the ill-feeling of the day. This tendency of hers may sometimes make it impossible for her to relax mentally, and the physical act can be somewhat mechanical when this happens. To a warm man such as this, such behavior could be misconstrued as frigidity.

Surprisingly enough, this relationship often works, due mainly to the constant challenge it offers.

Gemini Woman with Virgo Man

She will at first be attracted to Mr. Virgo's solid image, as it will represent security to her. She could also come to realize that here is a man who is willing to do any-thing for the girl he loves, who can provide mental stim-ulation and scope for her intelligence. Later, however, his sensible attitude and inability to fall in with her more unorthodox ideas will irritate her. His petty atti-tude towards money, too, will slowly breed resentment in her. The Virgo man wants to understand her sudden switches of mood, and may even feel that these are not quite normal—a reaction not likely to endear him to her. In moments of stress she may accuse him of being over-critical, cool and old-maidish, and in spells of de-pression he may find her too chaotic and vain.

Because of her lack of constancy in other things, he

soon begins to doubt her ability to love for any length of time and he becomes insecure. She, on the other hand, may become aggressive due to feelings of claustrophobia which he may unwittingly have created by his very insecurity.

Their sexual attraction for each other may be strong initially, but when Ms. Gemini feels her individuality threatened in any way she can turn off her physical desire for the offending person. And when he seems totally unconcerned about this, she could give up and look for comfort elsewhere.

This relationship is likely to be short-lived.

Gemini Woman with Libra Man

Both subjects here are born under Air signs and so they should have similar attitudes to feelings and intellect. An ideal situation should exist in their home when both partners are an equal force. The need for personal freedom is shared, as are the need for an active social life and a desire for constant change. He will perhaps want to lead his own life rather more than she does, and she will have to make him feel completely independent of her. His reluctance to help around the home could lead to nagging on her part and a quick exit by him. Displays of childish temper are thought unfeminine by Mr. Libra and although he may respond to her insecurity— brought about by jealousy—his sympathy will be lost if this gets out of control. But for most of the time their relationship should be rewarding as both partners believe that any union needs to be worked at constantly.

Mr. Libra is highly sexed and can provide as much mental stimulation as she can take. He will never cease wooing her and is naturally verbal in his admiration for her as a woman and an object of love, but it should be remembered that he will say exactly the same things to all his women, however convincing he may sound. He is usually a very proficient lover as he has much experience to draw from, so life could be one long ride on a merry-go-round; it could certainly never be dull.

A good union.

Gemini Woman with Scorpio Man

Mr. Scorpio has instincts which aid him in discovering immediately the nice things about her, but this has its disadvantages as he can almost certainly uncover the more unpleasant side of her personality. He, on the other hand, could remain a complete mystery to her as self-expression does not come easily to him. While Ms. Gemini tries to achieve a full and busy life, he is more concerned with attempting to improve himself. Tension may enter this union when he sees the delight she takes in stimulating company, as he is suspicious of other people and views them with a jealous eye. He sincerely wants to protect her and will show her how much he cares by action rather than words. Such a man needs a woman who is proud of him.

Although he may try hard to make her happy he often fails, because to the Gemini woman it is very important that she be continually involved in life and living. His jealousy can appall her and his possessiveness could create a feeling of imprisonment for her, one day making her feel emotionally secure, the next giving rise to thoughts of escape. The survival of this relationship is doubtful as two such different outlooks on life will rarely gel.

Many sexual partnerships are guided by events outside the bedroom, and this is a prime example. When moods do naturally coincide, making love will bring them closer together, but his insecurity could lead to violent, possibly physical, quarrels, from which he may seek refuge in drink. The Geminian is unlikely to put up with such treatment.

Not a good union.

Gemini Woman with Sagittarius Man

The Sagittarian man is full of fun, life and genuine love for his fellow man or woman—usually the latter. It is easy to fall in love with him but not so easy to make it last. He could be strongly attracted to Ms. Gemini as her need to converse, learn and observe is shared by him. Although it is well-hidden, she does have a strong practical streak which could clash with his ideas, for material considerations do not concern him. As both act as a magnet where people are concerned, their moments alone will be few.

Although both need personal freedom, they need it in vastly different ways. He must always feel free to do exactly as he pleases, while she will only want to do something when forbidden or restricted. He could respond to the feminine approach, but nagging is a sure way of driving him away. This individual will still shower attention on her long after they have met and will make no attempt to restrict her in any way, but his insistence on the plain unvarnished truth may hurt at times no matter how deeply her love goes, and if he is attracted to her girl-friends or has gone to bed with another woman he will tell her. In a strange way, she can respect such honesty.

Their sex life will be versatile and as a result anything could go. They may both break away for a weekend with another person, but wherever sex may lead them it will inevitably bring them back together again. A strong physical attraction is likely to exist between them.

A complex union.

Gemini Woman with Capricorn Man

Two characters more dissimilar would be hard to find, but the personalities can be made to complement each other. Mr. Capricorn is reserved, serious, practical and places much emphasis on his career. She would be wise to take an interest in his work, but if she cannot bring herself to share in his ambitions she will be shutting herself off from a very important part of his life. Ms. Gemini is a natural talker but she must force herself to listen to his problems as in this way he can ease the tension building up inside him. In return for such understanding he can still the restlessness that churns around inside of her. He is quite content to let her make a life for herself but he could share most of her interests in the aesthetic side of life.

Mr. Capricorn is urged on by a compelling desire to save and think of the future while Ms. Gemini may prefer to think of her present financial needs and no further. These are basic differences that should be acknowledged, for it will take much love to overcome them.

Sexually the union may work if she can learn how to take his mind off his career and all the problems associated with it, but this does entail generous effort and Ms. Gemini could consider this to be beneath her. Having to arouse male interest is something that is completely alien to her, for she has rarely needed to work at it in the past. Her ego may suffer when she realizes that he is lying next to her in bed working out some problem instead of giving his attention to her, and she may very well turn to someone else in an effort to re-establish her attractiveness as a woman.

A union bringing much hard work to those involved.

Gemini Woman with Aquarius Man

Mr. Aquarius is full of concern for the world, an incurable reformer. He may consider that she should drop whatever she is doing to listen to and converse with him on an intellectual level, at any time. Ms. Gemini will no doubt appreciate this excuse for dropping some uncongenial task. They will agree on a constant change of friends and interests, but she does not allow her outside affections to interfere with her personal relationships and she could become greatly agitated if he kept her waiting while he sorted out a friend's problem. He will not understand how such an adaptable girl could become so overwrought over such a trivial matter. Once committed to her, he becomes totally honest with her and shows an interest in everything she does. He then tends to see only the more pleasant side of her personality.

Outside interests may detract from the sexual side of their life together for both always have a lot going on around them, but assuming that they find the time no further mental stimulation should be necessary. There may be times when Ms. Gemini feels that perhaps they are missing something in their union, but in general she will be too busy to pursue this thought in any depth.

A good but not a physically based union.

Gemini Woman with Pisces Man

In this relationship there are in fact four personalities present, as both Ms. Gemini and Mr. Pisces have two sides to their character. Mr. Pisces can be logical, positive and bursting with ideas one day, and withdrawn, secretive and illogical the next. She may fall in love with one side of him, for his intuition and perceptiveness are attractive to her, and he is able to understand her every desire, but when the other side of his personality comes to the fore clashes can be expected. Ms. Gemini needs to understand the reason for anything he does where he would rather retire into a secret world where he can solve his problems or plan his next move on his own.

When he emerges she will, however, find that he has decided exactly what he wants next from life and how to get it. She will have to respect this side of him if problems are to be avoided.

She may be confused if his aggression disappears just when it is most needed, but if she starts to apply pressure it will be resented fiercely. This character needs a secure background and a devoted companion who will help him to become more resilient when life deals him a cruel blow. If she fails him he will not protest but will drift away.

Sexual compatibility should not be a problem in this case, for both need a strong shoulder on occasions and a keen sense of fun is apparent in both. He often tortures himself with strange fancies brought on by insecurity. His vivid imagination is often drawn to the eccentric or unusual sexual behavior of others. This can lead to stimulation by pornographic literature. It is essential that she avoid deluding herself into thinking that he will become stronger in time, rather she should be prepared to take the lead on many occasions or forget him.

A shaky union.

Gemini Woman with Aries Man

The Gemini woman could be impressed by this man's strength of character, independence and confidence; his quick decisive manner in love or business and his search for new ideas seem at first to be akin to her own personality. Mr. Aries will quickly assume the role of leader in their relationship and for a time this may appeal as a novel experience—until she realizes that he means it, then she could become bored. Further irritation comes from their different interests, for he does not share her enthusiasm for artistic pursuits, nor she his sports. Tempers will be released on some days but they both have short memories and in general arguments should be quickly forgotten, though his recovery is likely to be slower than her own. The Arietian way of showing affection could be too intense for Ms. Gemini and she could become detached as a result. If this should continue for any length of time he will conclude that she is unfeeling or cold. Mentally she is able to classify, dissect and file him away, but he will never understand her complex mind which can amuse or frustrate him depending on his mood.

Sexual problems may arise as he is unable to grasp her need for mental stimulation, to him this is all quite unnecessary. The rows which follow will develop a rift in their relationship. If she attempts to discuss this with him he could become arrogant and she may consider him uncouth and offensive.

Much give and take is needed if such a union is to survive.

Gemini Woman with Taurus Man

Both parties tend to indulge in romantic fancy on occasions, and while the Gemini woman is in this frame of mind she may be attracted to Mr. Taurus. His slow and conservative way of proceeding through life will eventually grate on her nerves, however, and his stubborn refusal to even consider change she will look on as shortsightedness. She can appreciate her home on occasions but cannot exist for it, she feels that life has more to offer, while he naturally expects her to assume a full-time domestic role and to be content with providing him with a comfortable background. Things could reach breaking point when he finally understands that she cannot be this type of woman. Although artistic activities can be shared this will not make up for deficiencies in other directions.

The sexual appetite of the Taurean is very well developed, but his direct approach could offend her. If he can control this tendency he may be able to arouse hidden feelings in her, but his jealousy can be all-consuming, causing her much suffering and driving her away from him. Sexually they may be well-matched but their approach to lovemaking is so vastly different as to make it almost impossible for them to successfully respond to each other.

Any relationship other than marriage is recommended.

ARE YOU A TYPICAL GEMINIAN MAN?

Answer honestly the questions below, using Yes, No or Sometimes, then turn to page 295 for the answer.

1. Are married or attached women irresistible to you?

2. Do you believe that you can make it with any woman if you really put your mind to it?

3. Are you attracted to a woman's mind in a lengthy relationship?

4. Are you a talkative man?

5. Do you loathe possessive women?

6. Could you be faithful to any one woman for life?

7. Can you be pretty crude in sex quite naturally?

8. Despite your swinging image do you harbor what may be considered some old-fashioned ideas?

9. Are you a jack-of-all-trades?

10. Are your moods changeable?

11. Are you self-critical?

12. Do you enjoy travel?

13. Is your curiosity insatiable?

14. Are you aroused sexually through your mind rather than through your body?

15. Do you discuss your sex life intimately with male friends?

16. Are you totally free of inhibition?

17. Does it make you feel good to have several women in love with you?

18. Do you prefer a stimulating conversation to a mediocre romp in bed?

19. Do you enjoy subjugating your women?

Score three for every Yes, two for every Sometimes and one for every No, then total up your score and turn to page 295 for your answer.

ARE YOU A TYPICAL GEMINIAN WOMAN?

Answer honestly the questions below, using Yes, No or Sometimes, then turn to page 296 for the answer.

1. Is mental stimulation important to you before sex?

2. When writing do your thoughts run ahead of your pen?

3. Do you suffer from extreme moods?

4. Are you talkative?

5. Do you have quick nervous mannerisms?

6. Does fantasy play an important role in your sex-life?

7. Do you use the words "I love you" a little too readily?

8. Would it really put you off to make love in silence?

9. Does the chase and challenge of a relationship stimulate you more than the actual sex act?

10. Do you rebel against routine?

11. Do you think you should feel more maternal than you do?

12. Do you believe that mental compatibility is the most important thing in a relationship?

13. Are you always attracted to the wrong people?

14. Do you feel claustrophobic when a man tries to possess you?

15. Are pretty speeches important to you when making love?

16. Do you take great delight in trying to shock?

17. Do you spend hours trying to dissect yourself?

18. Does insomnia plague you due to an over-active mind?

19. When making love does the use of four-letter words stimulate you?

20. Do you believe that making love is an art form?

Score three for Yes, two for Sometimes and one for No, then total your score and turn to page 296.

CANCER

THE CRAB

The Sign of the Prophet and Teacher

June 22nd to July 22nd

THE FIRST WATER SIGN: *Tenacious, patient, sensitive, sympathetic, changeable*

RULER: *Mercury*   GEMS: *Moss-agate, emerald*

COLOR: *Violet*   METAL: *Silver*

Characteristics of the Higher Male

The most prominent features of this type are adaptability, tenacity and patience; once an object has been seized he takes possession and like the crab would rather lose a claw than let go. This tendency is carried through from possessions to loved ones and ideas.

The highly developed male is a master of many moods, forever constant in his inconsistency. The whole range of emotion is at his fingertips, he can feel, and make others feel, joy, sorrow, horror and compassion. No other type can despair as can Mr. Cancer, whose vivid imagination can take hold of any emotion and intensify it. His memory is strong and retentive, the past very real to him—great importance is placed on the history of his family, nation or religion.

Dramatic by nature, he enjoys an audience and is attracted to a career that can supply one, however small —the schoolroom in many cases will fulfill this need— but when this is denied, his friends and family are resorted to for this purpose.

Affections are deep and lasting, no distance or period of time can lessen the family ties or dim a friendship. When he becomes a family man with a son, this bond will be a close one jealously guarded by the subject, and will prove his inspiration on many occasions. It is natural for this man to revolve his entire career and life around his loved ones; until this gap in his life is filled he may feel incomplete and will drift along influenced by everyone and everything around him. Unsympathetic discipline generally causes him intense suffering, and in any case proves quite useless for he follows his own will, if not openly then in secret, and the resentment aroused in him may distort his loving disposition against the disciplinarian. His imagination craves constant nourishment and shows itself in his love of history, books, drama and the cinema. When starved of these stimuli, morbid feelings can set in and he will become totally illogical and willful.

Because of his sensitivity, everything pertaining to his family is keenly felt and domestic ties can act as a kind of brake on the individual's progress. Loneliness is avoided wherever possible, his natural inclinations leading him into a clan or sect of sorts. The approval of others is eagerly sought and a fear of ridicule binds him closely to convention.

His ambition takes an unusual form for it is a love of fame and recognition that he seeks; this desire for power can lead to a high position which, once attained, is tenaciously clung to. It is rare for a Cancer man to fall from the top once he reaches it.

Characteristics of the Higher Female

This female shares all the vices and virtues of her brother, adding to them the ability to make an excellent mother, a maternal instinct being very much to the fore of her personality. If, however, she should be frustrated in this essential part of her character it could lead to withdrawal into her own dream world, a senseless drifting from one relationship to another, or she may become a drag on her family and friends, leaning heavily on their time and energy. Ms. Cancer is for the most happiest when married at an early age, for only in close partnership can she truly fulfill herself. Frequently, she turns to food for compensation and is as a result prone to overweight. Although her protective shell is desperately needed to assist her to survive the harder blows in life, she must try not to retire too deeply into it for there is a danger in that few human creatures possess the patience needed to coax her out.

Characteristics of the Lower Type

The lower individual becomes a slave rather than a master to his moods. He over-indulges in sentimentalism, sensationalism and exaggerated emotion of every kind and is a bundle of contradictions and inconsistencies. His own importance is blown out of all proportion, losing the sympathy and the friendship of others.

This type must attract attention no matter to what extremes he may have to go; as a notorious hypochondriac, health can sometimes be effectively used to achieve this end. Fierce pride and independence alternate with helplessness and loneliness, there are weeks when he avoids his fellow men while he indulges in bouts of self-pity, morbid thoughts and depressions, from which he eventually emerges only to resume his attempt to attract the limelight for himself. When badly afflicted, his sexual desires can become masochistic.

Physical Characteristics

In structure the Cancer subject's frame is large and bony, arms are long in proportion to the body, feet and hands tend to be big and the skull is generous with a pronounced lower jaw. The mouth is wide, expressing clearly all the emotions. The nose as a rule is turned-up,

eyes are wide apart—often shortsighted—and the eyebrows have a distinct downward curve.

The stomach and breasts are ruled by this sign and
much attention needs to be paid to diet if irritations are
to be avoided. Worry can result in indigestion which
may in turn produce defective circulation, and a tendency to always fear the worst does not help the subject. An over-active imagination inclines this type to
vivid nightmares.

CANCER MALE

	Sex	Love	Marriage	Business	Friends (opposite sex)	Friends (same sex)
ARIES						
TAURUS		•	•	•	•	
GEMINI					•	
CANCER	•				•	
LEO						
VIRGO				•		•
LIBRA	•				•	
SCORPIO		•	•	•	•	•
SAGITTARIUS						
CAPRICORN	•					
AQUARIUS	•				•	
PISCES	•	•	•			•

CANCER FEMALE

	Sex	Love	Marriage	Business	Friends (opposite sex)	Friends (same sex)
ARIES						
TAURUS		•	•	•	•	•
GEMINI						
CANCER	•				•	
LEO						
VIRGO	•		•	•		•
LIBRA	•					
SCORPIO		•	•		•	•
SAGITTARIUS						
CAPRICORN				•	•	
AQUARIUS	•	•		•	•	
PISCES		•	•			•

CANCER MAN tends to have a medium build with large hands and feet; a large skull with an overhanging brow and a pronounced lower jaw; a turned-up nose.

CANCER WOMAN tends to have a long body with a good bust and large hips and thighs; large feet; a strong jaw; shortsighted or deep-set eyes; a pale skin.

THE CANCER PARTNERSHIPS

Cancer Woman with Cancer Man

Two domestic, romantic and sensitive people should be able to use these mutual characteristics as a good basis for a happy relationship. Excess sensitivity, however, can lead to trouble. Every word and action taken so literally can mean consistent hurt for one or both of them, and a serious problem could completely floor them. Both parties see themselves as the all-giving martyr and will be shocked when this is not recognized by the other. Mr. and Ms. Cancer both possess a retentive memory and the causes of quarrels are brought up again and again. Much time is wasted on petty bickering and dredging up the past. If they can detach themselves unemotionally from their relationship and look at it with a clear head they may see that they have much to be grateful for. When arguments do occur, however, they will both be quick to offer a reconciliation. Both personalities are highly complex and emotional and should try to view life with a more realistic eye.

Sexually the intricate feelings of both could cause trouble, for the occasions when desires coincide could be all too rare. This, coupled with the tendency of each partner to expect the other to adapt, makes for plenty of drama.

Cancer Woman with Leo Man

Mr. Leo can feel just as deeply about things as Ms. Cancer but this is often hidden behind a proud and arrogant facade. He likes to be the dominating force in their relationship and cannot see any reason to continually give in to her. Both partners are inclined to sulk when things do not go as planned and this could lead to days of silence. In spite of these faults, when he finally gives he will give whole-heartedly, and if sensible she will try to be everything he could possibly want in a woman, for she can instinctively provide the kind of home that he needs and this may heal many a sore wound. He usually, however, devotes some considerable time to a sport and she would be well advised to take an interest in it or be prepared to feel left out or ill-used. This man expects to receive admiration and respect from her. Mr. Leo periodically becomes wildly extravagant, thus offending her economical virtue. Worries regarding the future only amuse him and are totally incomprehensible to his mind. Given time they may be able to influence one another although neither personality is adaptable enough to effect a permanent change.

Sexually their appetites vary considerably; she may eventually decide that his demands are excessive. The Cancer woman expects a sensitive and loving approach where the Leo man can sometimes be quite basic; he often resorts to four-letter words in an effort to express the passion he is feeling.

This relationship should only be entered into with eyes wide open, or chances of success will diminish rapidly.

Cancer Woman with Virgo Man

Mr. Virgo is ruled by his intellect and logic, and these qualities can make him quite a formidable force. While Ms. Cancer may wish she could be more outgoing, her emotions inevitably frustrate this desire. Her domestic talents will, however, be well appreciated by this man and will make him feel secure, but the continual presence of friends and particularly relatives in their home may irritate him, for his ties with his family are not as close as hers. Although shrewd in financial matters the Cancer woman cannot be as critical as he is in this direction. There is a danger in this relationship as both enjoy looking after and fussing around those they love, eventually making life intolerable for both of them. In general, they both need a more positive partner so that instead of constant discussion on what needs to be done some action takes place.

Sex is unlikely to play a major role in this partnership as neither person is greatly motivated by this urge. It will, however, provide a tender and gentle side to their life together.

Petty quarrels are likely to spoil the harmony within this relationship.

Cancer Woman with Libra Man

Mr. Libra can enjoy the domestic side of life provided this is not pushed on to him. He needs wider horizons to function properly. Decision-making could be difficult in this relationship as he procrastinates while she avoids it altogether. He enjoys the challenge of making a partnership work and will put much effort into it. This man is well acquainted with female desires and knows exactly what she wants at any given time. Ms. Cancer will need to develop her intellect, however, if she is to keep this gay character interested for he grows restless and bored easily, and her martyr complex could be hard for him to take. She may eventually learn to relax and enjoy life a little more, and he could come to appreciate her devotion.

Physically it could be hard for her to hold this man's attention as his eyes constantly look for greener pastures. She will have to remain glamorous in and out of bed to achieve this. Sex is an important part of his make-up, so she could be busy keeping up with him in this direction. Her preference for the romantic or loving approach is just not stimulating enough for the Libra man. He may be stimulated by the thought of various sexual perversions whereas she will feel revolted.

A tense relationship.

Cancer Woman with Scorpio Man

Both of these subjects are motivated by emotion and intuition. The bond they share will usually be exceptionally strong. He loves whole-heartedly, insists on fidelity, is a good provider, and keeps a jealous eye on their relationship. Fortunately, Ms. Cancer will never give him reason to suspect or mistrust her as her beliefs are in accordance with his. He works hard and needs a comfortable home in which to relax and recover from his daily exertions. Although he will not look at another woman, he will expect to find everything feminine in her. There are occasions, however, when her natural concern for others may tend to make him think the worst of them, especially those who pay her considerable attention. Ms. Cancer, although naturally critical, has great respect for this man and knows exactly how to phrase her complaints.

Sexually, he can possess her completely, making her feel very precious and inspiring response far greater than she would normally be capable of with another type of man. Her usual loving approach to sex is widened in this relationship—she is able to express herself more freely and become more passionate.

An excellent partnership.

Cancer Woman with Sagittarius Man

If this relationship is to even remotely work both partners will need to enjoy fighting, for rows and arguments are bound to come in plenty. She must be prepared to live life fully with him and not drift into vegetation. Mr. Sagittarius prefers to lead a very active and social life and he will expect her to come along with him. On the occasions when she wishes to stay at home, eat a good meal and watch the television, he will try to persuade her to join him in going out. When he fails, he will leave on his own in a search for excitement elsewhere. Love to the Sagittarian man does not mean he cannot see and flirt with other women; when he does this, the dramatic way Ms. Cancer reacts will only make him feel he has made a mistake in choosing her. This is a generous and lucky man, full of charm, so much so that she may get used to his ideas on freedom. If, however, she finds these totally unacceptable, a friendship with him may prove less nerve-racking than a closer bond.

Sexually Mr. Sagittarius is very active and, though her desires are more easily satisfied, he may persuade her that she has been missing an awful lot in the bedroom. Although he may be a little impatient with her routine approach, he is expert enough to see this as a challenge and could be successful in rousing her more animal instincts.

A love-hate relationship.

Cancer Woman with Capricorn Man

When Ms. Cancer gets involved with this man she should automatically prepare to accept his career. This he assumes she will naturally do. But this woman demands much of his attention and may regard him as a

bore when observing his absorption in his occupation.
Mr. Capricorn may feel that she should channel her
sensitive and emotional instincts into her own career,
thus making her less dependent upon him. Financial
problems are unlikely to occur for both are good with
money. Earning a living comes naturally to him as does
his ability to save. Waste of any kind deeply offends this
man and extravagant impulses should be checked. This
is a faithful and devoted man, and she should be content with him.

His career can interfere with their sex life, for he may
enjoy studying or reading his papers in bed. If she is
clever she could slip an erotic book into his work re-
ports, trusting he will take the hint.

A relationship that needs a lot of hard work.

Cancer Woman with Aquarius Man

Mr. Aquarius could be initially attracted to Ms. Cancer's sensitive and domestic personality, but he loves to
improve everything around him and this will include
her. The tenacious side of her personality is unlikely to
approve of this. She is proud of her intuition and he of
his logic; disagreement is inevitable because of this. She
may feel that she has constantly to tempt him to come
home and spend some time with her, for he will invariably be with friends, exchanging ideas or helping them
in some way.

The Aquarian man believes the truth to be all-important. This may be misconstrued by her, she may feel
justified in airing her own grievances—and he could

then find himself bearing the brunt of her complaints and nagging.

Sexual appetites are evenly balanced, but she will need to learn how to entice him into bed before he can find something better to do. She can learn how to stimulate him mentally through discussion; she may be able to turn the subject around to sex and obtain some response from him physically.

This relationship is likely to be of short duration.

Cancer Woman with Pisces Man

Both people in this relationship possess strong imaginative and instinctive powers. It should therefore be easy for them to understand each other with a minimum of trouble. The need for emotional security is paramount in both, this together with a little effort can create a close relationship. Mr. Pisces has a love of all vulnerable beings and she could find their home filled with stray dogs, cats or any poor creatures without a home.

His sudden pessimistic moods, brought on for no apparent reason, are often instigated by some petty matter. At this time he needs much love and understanding plus all the optimism she can muster. There are many occasions when she may feel that the world takes him for granted, although he can feel the same about her. This man needs much looking after for he is inclined to overindulge in depression, drinking and smoking, although this should be done with the minimum of fuss. The maternal instinct being strong in Ms. Cancer, there will be many occasions when she can happily put it to use.

Sexually, the imagination could play an important part, for this is a side of their nature which is well developed—although it is more likely to be put to use in a romantic way. A strong physical attraction is likely to exist between them, however, and their sex life should serve to build on their already solid union.

Cancer Woman with Aries Man

Although very different from this man, Ms. Cancer could be so overpowered by his strong personality that before she knows what has happened she could be deeply involved with him. But before long she will notice just how different their values in life are. He continually searches for fresh scope and activity while she desires a quiet and restful existence. To her his love seems to burn so fiercely that she begins to doubt how long such intensity can last. Later still, he may come to realize that he has been blinded by passion and that in fact Ms. Cancer cannot keep up with him, and he could begin to show signs of restlessness. He cannot understand feminine moods and will make no attempt to try. She may decide that love does not mean the same to him as it does to herself.

In order to make a success of this partnership she must attempt to become more resilient and open-minded, while he must keep a tight rein on his "me first" impulses, and try to consider her feelings more.

Sexually, Ms. Cancer's need for a romantic and loving approach is completely disregarded by this man, these characteristics being alien to his personality. Mr. Aries is aggressive in love, and if the tension outside the bedroom filters into their sex life his sadistic streak could come to the fore, horrifying and mortifying her.

Where one personality is so complex and the other so direct it would be hard to achieve harmony.

Cancer Woman with Taurus Man

The mutual desire for a domestic and steady background could well be the reason for the attraction between these two characters. He will enjoy the attention given to him when arriving home after an exhausting day at work, and her ability to serve him a tempting meal will appeal to one of the softer spots in his personality. His possessive streak has little reason to exercise itself in this relationship for she will be totally devoted to him and him alone. The neurotic tendencies that surface in her with a more volatile man are quietened here and channeled into the building of a home and into making life as pleasant as possible for them. The biggest danger to them could be that life may settle down into an unimaginative and boring routine, and she should guard against becoming too humdrum.

Although initially their sexual relationship could really swing, after a short period of time it may deteriorate into an unexciting act performed automatically, but although conservative Mr. Taurus can be highly sexed, and she should try to prevent boredom creeping in by use of her vivid imagination.

Cancer Woman with Gemini Man

Mr. Gemini's zest for living, charm and gift of communication could all initially appeal to Ms. Cancer, although at the back of her mind she may feel that they are basically very different. This will become more apparent as time passes. He cannot stay in one spot or pursue one train of thought for any length of time, he needs constant novelty and stimulation in order to function properly. Such erratic behavior cannot fail to intrude upon the quiet and domestic atmosphere she prefers. Her strong tendency to cling to love objects could have a disastrous effect on the Gemini man, for he is elusive and will not be possessed in any way.

Like her, he is a moody person, but his moods are changeable and basically quite superficial whereas hers are far deeper and it is not easy for her to lift herself out of them. He could therefore be quite irritated when she seems to be deliberately set in one frame of mind, not realizing that it is he who can change this.

Although not unfaithful without good reason, the Gemini man does enjoy the company of women and can flirt outrageously at the slightest provocation. This is mostly instigated by the need to assure his masculine ego and to dig beneath the surface of anyone he meets. When this does occur he could be faced with an emotional scene, for Ms. Cancer is likely to place more importance on this than is warranted.

Where once more Ms. Cancer can only respond to

emotion and love where sex is concerned, he can only be stimulated by his present state of mind. If her response to sex is always constant it will not be long before this man is looking for variety elsewhere.

The opposing personalities could make this a very difficult relationship.

ARE YOU A TYPICAL CANCERIAN MAN?

Answer honestly the questions below using Yes, No or Sometimes, then turn to page 297 for the answer.

1. Are you protective with those you love?

2. Does the sea attract you?

3. Do you long for a large family?

4. Is a drink with the boys important to you?

5. Does the idea of being in bed with two women appeal?

6. Do you place your women on pedestals?

7. Do you keep letters from old lovers?

8. Is your memory retentive?

9. Do you work slowly and carefully?

10. Do you secretly enjoy having dependents?

11. Is it hard for you to suggest new ideas or new ways of making love?

12. Do you believe in one affair at a time?

13. Do you participate in some kind of sport?

14. Does travel attract you?

15. Do you care how others see you?

16. Do you think that the permissive society has gone too far?

17. Do you enjoy being in the limelight?

18. Is it hard for you to recover when a deep relationship ends?

19. When others smirk at sentiment or romance are you annoyed?

20. Do you expect your woman to revolve her life around you?

Total up your score, allowing three for every Yes, two for every Sometimes and one for every No, and turn to page 297.

ARE YOU A TYPICAL CANCERIAN WOMAN?

Answer the questions below using Yes, No, or Sometimes, and then turn to page 298 for your answer.

1. When watching a film or reading a book are the impressions you receive from them hard to shake off afterwards?

2. Does the romantic side of history appeal to you?

3. Do you think marriage is incomplete without children?

4. Is it difficult for you to stay with an unfaithful man?

5. Are you self-protective?

6. Do you feel uncomfortable at the thought of taking the lead in bed?

7. Is a martyr complex part of your personality?

8. Do you enjoy the limelight in any form?

9. Are you easily hurt?

10. Does the sea attract you?

11. Do you take your sexual affairs seriously?

12. Have you a weight problem?

13. Are you influenced greatly by those around?

14. Is it hard for you to have more than one sexual affair in progress at a time?

15. Do you suffer from morbid thoughts and moods?

16. Do you lose those you love because of your tendency to cling?

17. Are you good with money?

18. Do you dread being alone?

19. Do antiques interest you?

20.   Are your sex fantasies mostly romantic?

Total up your score, allowing three for every Yes, two for every Sometimes and one for every No, and turn to page 298.

LEO

THE LION

The Sign of the King or President

July 23rd to August 23rd

THE SECOND FIRE SIGN: *Proud, generous, trusting, energetic, domineering, authoritative, warmhearted.*

RULER: *The Sun* **GEMS:** *Ruby, diamond*

COLOR: *Orange* **METAL:** *Gold*

Characteristics of the Higher Male

The Leo man, whether he is tall or short, can never be overlooked, his very presence commands attention. His regal bearing and good appearance can usually guarantee this. His clothing is a source of much talk amongst

friends due either to its flamboyance or expensive appearance. He is a man who cannot fail to impress for
good or evil on first meeting.

This subject makes an ideal head of any enterprise.
Many-sided himself, he understands and appreciates
the different qualities of other types and rarely wastes
time or energy asking from anyone what it is not in his
or her power to give. Commands, to be effective, must
be easily understood and therefore his style is simple
and straightforward; approval is definite and unmistakable, displeasure intimated without hesitation or cir-
cumlocution.

The past is held in reverence, the future looked forward to with the faith and optimism of a child. Shining
as a host, he delights in giving of his best to guests and
strangers. The emotions of this type tend to be over-
generous and too widespread; his characteristic faith
often leads to misplaced affections and unwise relationships. But his magnanimity and power of forgiveness
can frequently bring success out of failure or enable him
to adjust himself to almost impossible conditions. Mr.
Leo is capable of enduring much work but his method
is erratic and exasperating for those around; he will toil
without rest for a period of time and then, quite suddenly, relapse into an utterly lazy phase during which
time he will be immovable, stirring only when he deems
himself ready to carry on.

This individual makes a wonderful, warm and open
friend, nothing is too good or too much trouble for
those he loves, and when he marries Mr. Leo is an excellent provider. Being at the center of the fire triplicity,
he possesses a strong love nature which makes him ar-

dent and sincere in affections. Because his emotional force springs directly from the heart, the Leo man feels deeply, often resorting to arrogance in an effort to hide his sensitivity.

No sign can equal the pride of this type, many of his actions or lack of actions are guided by this, and when his vanity is wounded he can suffer so considerably that his health may be impaired. The love of luxury is intense, often acting as a spur to his ambition, for he appreciates all the good things in life.

His sexual appetite is well developed and this makes sex of paramount importance to him, much thought goes into affairs and he abandons himself heart and soul into each experience. Women are very attracted to this man, they sense his masculinity and love of everything feminine. His generosity and warmth, endowed on him by the Sun, radiates from him to all with whom he comes into contact. The weakness in his personality is a love of flattery and admiration: both are needed desperately, and any female with designs on this man should remember that flattery will get her everywhere.

Characteristics of the Higher Female

The female of the sign is very similar to her male counterpart, she too makes a wonderful friend, has fierce pride and takes naturally to the good things in life. Clothes are of consequence, jewelry treasured, often collected, and a lot of money is spent on her appearance.

Although her sex-drive is strong, the procedure for

her necessitates comfort and ease: no back seat of a car or cinema for her. The unshakable faith she possesses seems all too frequently to be placed in the wrong people and she suffers unnecessary heartache because of this. Broken engagements, separations and divorce are as a rule to be found in her past. Her judgment is too easily deceived by appearance and her desire for comfort can lead to her entertaining the idea of marriage for material reasons but should this in fact become a reality, failure would be almost unavoidable for this is a woman who feels deeply and needs to love constantly to remain well-balanced.

Characteristics of the Lower Type

The lower Leo is cursed with an unquenchable thirst for personal glory, he is ambitious for responsible and high positions which if acquired he would be totally incapable of filling with success. He assumes airs of self-importance, trying to lord it over whoever he considers to be his inferior, and he attempts to get too far too soon, losing all through lack of experience, laziness or restlessness.

His biggest weakness is favoritism, selecting colleagues and friends for their ability to flatter and feed his ego rather than for their talents or warmth. Many of this type seek to marry beneath them, trying to ensure that they can at least feel superior to someone. The lower Leo is incapable of judging character through anything other than appearance and is much impressed by outward wealth. His sexual appetite is insatiable and uncontrollable. The subject when very weak will arrive at all sexual deviation at some time or other.

Physical Characteristics

The Leo is recognized by his regal bearing, deliberation of speech or movement and his generously sized skull. Most subjects of this sign are inclined to be tall in stature, but even a small Leo cannot be overlooked in a crowd. He is well-proportioned, has a light step with a stride longer than the average, and his laughter will frequently resemble a roar. Dancing may be popular with him for he possesses a natural grace.

In health matters Leo is either exceptionally strong, radiating vitality all around him, or forever on the sick list. Discordant and unharmonious environments, hurt pride and unrequited love can all react on health. His best medicine is peace, love and harmony.

LEO MALE

	Sex	Love	Marriage	Business	Friends (opposite sex)	Friends (same sex)
ARIES		•	•	•	•	•
TAURUS						
GEMINI	•	•	•	•		•
CANCER						
LEO	•			•	•	
VIRGO						
LIBRA	•					
SCORPIO						
SAGITTARIUS		•		•		•
CAPRICORN						
AQUARIUS					•	
PISCES	•					

LEO FEMALE

	Sex	Love	Marriage	Business	Friends (opposite sex)	Friends (same sex)
ARIES		•	•	•	•	•
TAURUS						
GEMINI	•	•	•	•	•	•
CANCER						
LEO	•			•	•	•
VIRGO	•					
LIBRA					•	•
SCORPIO	•					
SAGITTARIUS		•	•	•	•	•
CAPRICORN				•		
AQUARIUS						
PISCES	•					

LEO MAN tends to have a long, powerful body with short legs and strong hands; a large skull with thick, silky hair and a square jaw; warm, light eyes.

LEO WOMAN tends to have a long body with short legs, and a proud bearing; a wide skull with large eyes, small ears and nose and a short neck.

THE LEO PARTNERSHIPS

Leo Woman with Leo Man

Identical personalities can in some cases be a good basis for a relationship, but when both characters are strong and inflexible, as in this instance, trouble cannot be far off. The Leo man must always be the leader, but he will have to fight for this position with Ms. Leo, as she cannot take the orders that this man can unthinkingly issue, and mutual jealousy can aggravate an already tense situation. The career is important to both of them, which could lead to a sense of competition developing between them. Generally Mr. Leo is attracted to a feminine woman and this aggressive streak in Ms. Leo he could consider unnatural. He demands to be the center of her existence and will not be put aside for ambitions. No sign, however, is more generous or warm, the ability to love is also great, and these traits may help to ease the situation somewhat. They share a love of ostentation and show, and much pleasure may be derived from making their home a showplace for all to admire. In general, when in the hands of a Leo man monetary affairs are unsettled, for he is inclined to gamble with life using all or nothing as his odds. But with two Leos contributing, when one of his gigantic enterprises fails hopelessly, then maybe one of hers will be paying off.

As a rule Leo confers on its subjects a strong sex drive, therefore in this union much time may be spent in bed and many a domestic quarrel solved there. The physical attraction should be inescapable, the wants, needs and desires shared. This can lead to an overactive sex life which may develop in various directions as sex can be separated totally from love. Infidelity may be tolerated provided honesty is observed.

An intense love or hate relationship.

Leo Woman with Virgo Man

The need for constant flattery could have been unfilled at the time of meeting this man, and while going through a rare phase of inferiority she could be attracted to characteristics which do not normally appeal to her. Mr. Virgo loves to help anyone in trouble, but once she has regained her self-confidence he will be confronted with a totally different woman. Attitudes to money differ vastly, he budgets, saves, and spends grudgingly, offending the generosity of Ms. Leo. Her own attitude to money is spend now and worry about it later. When she buys an extravagant outfit to boost her morale his cool reaction and cutting tongue could deeply hurt her.

The different approaches to recreation can also cause friction for to him relaxing is a waste of time while it plays an important part in her life. She loves to entertain and nothing is too good for the people she loves, and Mr. Virgo—left paying the bills—could become most unpleasant.

Approaches to work vary considerably; he may work hard and conscientiously for fourteen hours a day with little appreciation or material gain, where in half the time she may accomplish recognition and much financial benefit. To make the relationship work at all, tolerance is needed on both sides; he must learn to open his mind and horizons and she must realize that he is a perfectionist only trying to do his best for both of them.

Sexually, she could be in for a frustrating time for her warmth and love need constant expression and he is unlikely to appreciate this need, his own needs finding outlet in work, and her demands will go unheard or unanswered. The Leo woman is generous in love; she will give and give, but will eventually expect something back. Mr. Virgo on the other hand finds it difficult to express his needs or appreciate her efforts. This normally strong woman out of bed expects to be dominated when it comes to making love, but Mr. Virgo will find it difficult to respond to her demands.

A difficult and ill-advised relationship.

Leo Woman with Libra Man

Although basically two exceptionally warm personalities, character is likely to be incompatible in this instance. The Leo woman enjoys and believes in a good argument, feeling that this clears the air and eases tension. Mr. Libra, however, lives for harmony in all things and finds ugly outbursts uncongenial and unbalanced. When attempting to discuss disagreements calmly and clearly he will run up against the fiery Leo temper. Unless they are able to find some solution to this difference life is likely to be difficult. Decision-making can also provoke friction, for he will not face it until it is absolutely necessary, and she will accuse him of irresponsibility and an uncaring attitude.

The Libran man is inevitably drawn to beauty. This is particularly noted by her when an attractive woman is around, for he will instinctively flirt and attempt to charm the opposite sex whenever possible. This is especially true if there is an age difference in the relationship, for he worries about losing his youth and needs to reassure himself of his attractiveness.

Both personalities work erratically, they are both capable of extreme hard work but are equally able to indulge in long periods of inactivity. Despite this, it is unlikely that either will recognize this mutual trait and each could accuse the other of laziness.

Sexually, their appetites are about equal but very different. He needs glamour and fantasy and looks to her to supply it, but her own approach is more generous and straightforward. She cannot understand his need for stimulation through fantasy, and should he realize this his eye will begin to look for satisfaction elsewhere.

This relationship should be avoided whenever possible.

Leo Woman with Scorpio Man

Ms. Leo's generous, candid and outspoken manner does not mean that she wishes to reveal everything about herself, and when she finds herself under the critical Scorpio eye there will be fiery objections. Mr. Scorpio tends to dissect anybody he comes into contact with, although he can be very secretive himself, and will display outraged indignation when his own personality comes under her scrutiny. Mr. Scorpio finds it difficult to find a suitable partner and when he does he could be accused of being over-demanding. He expects total fidelity, a woman free from a career with no ambitious thoughts for herself, but expects her to be totally absorbed in his own activities. Ms. Leo's need for an individual life can only result in his insecurity and bitterness. Her natural aptitude for spending money can offend the Scorpio who will spasmodically spend money but likes to dictate the how and the when of expenses. If she can learn to appreciate the fighter and protector in him together with the security he offers, and if he can learn to value the warmth and ability to give in her, then life may not be too disastrous for them.

Sexually, as in all, Ms. Leo gives, and when she notices the reluctance on his part to do the same she could feel hurt, not realizing that self-expression comes hard to him. But his sexual appetite is likely to be over-active and in time this may compensate for some of the deficiencies elsewhere.

A very stormy relationship.

Leo Woman with Sagittarius Man

In this relationship Ms. Leo will seem to have found the right man to give all of her warmth and generosity to, for he can recognize the value of this and give in return. What she may not realize, however, is that he gives to everybody, though not necessarily for long. Her big heart could be badly bruised when he explains his views on individual freedom and need for harmless flirtations. He will enjoy her support when some crazy gamble appeals as a chance to make big money, and when this goes wrong will be grateful for the love shown instead of recriminations. Interests may differ for he is an outdoor enthusiast where she prefers her pleasures in comfort, but again it should not be hard to come to some agreement without either side appearing to have given in. Should she prefer to concentrate on her career rather than totally on him, his free from jealous nature will encourage and spur her on, for he does not believe that any person should be dependent upon another.

Sexually, she should make no attempt to tame him. If she can learn to accept his occasional indiscretion he will always return to her and may eventually decide that there is no reason to look elsewhere for feminine company. His occasional wish to experiment or bring other people into their sexual activities should not be discouraged, rather if she is wise she could lead him to believe that one day she just might go along with this.

In this way she can retain his interest without appearing to restrict him in any way.

A rewarding relationship.

Leo Woman with Capricorn Man

One of the main reasons for conflict here could be their opposing materialistic attitudes. Ms. Leo enjoys extravagant clothes, furniture and is attracted to the status symbols of life where Mr. Capricorn has no need of any of life's trimmings and is more concerned with saving for their future. It will seem to him that even a simple trip to the cinema costs him a fortune for everything she does has to be done in style.

This man can when under pressure feel the sudden urge to break away and be by himself. She could be panic-stricken on awakening one morning to find that he has disappeared, and after a few days when she has contacted the police, his family and all of their friends, he will turn up quite unconcerned and refuse to understand why she is so upset.

Outlooks on life may also be incompatible as Ms. Leo is ever optimistic whereas Mr. Capricorn can rarely see the brighter side of life. Humor is probably called for at this point. She may be hurt when he does not notice a new hairstyle or dress, but neither will he notice when she is not looking her best or when time begins to take its toll.

Although straightforward, she can approach sex in a lighthearted frame of mind, but he is invariably rather straightfaced and serious. If she can stop herself draw-

ing attention to this, however, in time he may learn to
relax a little more. Further trouble may develop over
her wish at times to over-indulge in sex, for Mr. Capricorn believes in moderation in all things.

A shaky relationship.

Leo Woman with Aquarius Man

Ms. Leo could find Mr. Aquarius' detached aloofness a
challenge at first, for she will firmly believe that there is
a warmer personality beneath his exterior, but although
with time he may respond to her wholehearted give he
can never be as generous with himself as she is, and this
she must accept. Two characteristics are shared in this
relationship: fixed opinions and pride. These could be
the cause of many a quarrel. Where he is a humanitar-
ian, overlooking materialistic gain for the sake of ideals, financial success is inclined to come first with her
and she feels his ideas are unrealistic, although when he
returns home disillusioned and bitter she is the first to
offer love and consolation, checking the impulse to say
"I told you so." She will soon realize that to this man
she must be a companion first and a lover second. She
will need to share in the new interests which constantly
appeal to his imagination.

If the Aquarian man is of the lower type, violent
quarrels may take place, for where Ms. Leo is not afraid
to fight for what she wants in life the lower Aquarian is
guilty of cowardice, so that any opposition he is confronted with will find him backing away. This will only
need to occur once for the Leo woman to lose all her

respect for him, and if this happens it can only be a matter of time before they part company.

They may not spend much time in bed together, for he can always find an alternative to charm away his interest, which at times must frustrate her. He could think her over-demanding while she will feel he is inhuman.

Generally speaking, there is too much against this partnership for it to succeed, unless they both have a lot of sheer determination.

Leo Woman with Pisces Man

Ms. Leo may be attracted to this man because he seems in dire need of her protection, and then she will be greatly surprised when he suddenly becomes positive and full of action. To live with such an unstable character could have drastic effects on her, for the Leo woman usually likes to know where she stands. On occasions her generous love is received and reciprocated, on others he suddenly withdraws and mentally shuts her off while absorbed in the solving of some problem. In her loneliness she may throw herself into wild social activity which will irritate him during his need for peace and quiet. She may apply logic one day and an appeal to his emotions the next, but unless she can lodge these appeals at the appropriate time in his circle of ever-changing moods she will merely end up frustrated, confused and deeply hurt. Although Ms. Leo may brood when under stress, she does not sink into the black depressions that Mr. Pisces can experience at the drop of a hat. Eventually she could lose patience with what she considers unreasonable behavior and resort to arrogant self-protection, and when this happens he will completely cut her off, mentally and physically.

These changeable moods must reflect into the bedroom, but the oversexed Leo woman could find it easier to cope with them here. Sex means much to both parties and the relationship could well stand or fall on their bedroom activities. If she can honestly accept a weaker man then things may work out fine, otherwise he will bring her much unhappiness when falling short of her expectations.

A complex union.

Leo Woman with Aries Man

The Arietian confidence could hold great attraction for the Leo woman. He seems to be constantly involved in a fight with life and earns her respect. His impulsive streak, however, may worry her for in most things she prefers to take her time and consider before acting. The egos of both are exceptionally sensitive, she needs plenty of admiration and praise and he needs her encouragement in all his business activities, and when either ego is threatened they can become overbearing and violent, and dramatic quarrels will take place. Their life could deteriorate into a constant battle of wills, but if her pride can allow her to she should occasionally let him feel he has won. In this particular relationship argument can play an important part, for both personalities enjoy a fight. Although he will not object to any ambitions she may have connected with her career, he must never be made to believe it is more important to her than his own or himself.

Life could be difficult if financial problems exist for each has a well-developed sense for the full comforts of life and they can suffer considerably when forced to go without. It is unlikely that his financial ability will save the day and so it may be up to her to be a little more careful and practical.

The aggressive traits in both, plus Mr. Aries' slightly sadistic streak, could find outlet in bed, especially after one of their fiery arguments, for he may enjoy making love to her while hating her at the same time. They should be sexually compatible, but their sex life could burn itself out if imagination is not used to keep it alive.

A very fiery relationship.

Leo Woman with Taurus Man

Generally speaking, Ms. Leo is a confident and self-sufficient woman, but in her weaker moments Mr. Taurus could seem like an attractive proposition. His strength of character and common sense may seem a relief, especially if she has been recently involved with a weaker personality. This relationship could well start on the rebound for her. Normally a conservative and sober individual, he could in time respond to her outgoing nature and become more interested in the outside world. Stubbornness in personal opinions could be their main stumbling block. If either party believes himself to be right nothing will change his mind and very serious repercussions could be felt. They should only begin their relationship if they have no desire to change one another, for two less adaptable people would be hard to find. A horror of debt drives Mr. Taurus on to achieve financial security but the Taurean can never be secure enough and the extravagance notorious in the Leo will have to be curbed or she will be faced with an unbelievable display of temper. However, interest in the home, career and entertaining friends will be mutually enjoyed.

If she has been unfortunate enough to attract the lower type of Taurean his stubbornness, utter laziness and gluttony will be more than she can take, this together with his consuming jealousy can be relied upon to force this normally loyal woman into another's bed.

The Taurean may be prone to sexual over-indulgence, but as the Leo's own appetite is not inconsiderable this should not cause any problems. While their sex life will be straightforward, it could be most satisfactory, but in this particular relationship it is what occurs outside of the bedroom that really counts.

A normally incompatible combination of characters.

Leo Woman with Gemini Man

Although sometimes realistic and sensible where matters of the heart are concerned, Ms. Leo can be very impulsive and Mr. Gemini, who is forever involved in some new game of love, is happy to go along with her. They could be deeply involved in a very short space of time. The Geminian will introduce much activity and interest and will involve her in a hectic social life. Superficially their relationship could work very well, but eventually the wish to dominate in Ms. Leo will exercise itself. The Gemini man may not take this seriously at first but when he realizes she plans to take him over and run his life he will rebel and probably leave. It could be very difficult for this woman to hang on to her Geminian for long; she does not understand his need for mental stimulation, his desire to communicate with many different kinds of people or to be constantly involved in new things. Although impressed by her fiery displays of love and at times drawing security from them, in general he will feel smothered by such intense emotion. Often a vicious circle is set up where the more he pulls away from her the more she will try to possess, until little is left of the great love they started out with.

Sexually, he needs a lot of stimulation, fantasy and experimentation, which on the whole she will find confusing, for her own desire can be aroused quite easily. If she can learn to be a little more unconventional in her lovemaking and realize it does not always have to happen in bed, then maybe things will work out.

As a general rule, the pressure put upon these two individuals through trying to live together will destroy the partnership.

Leo Woman with Cancer Man

The Leo woman could be instantly drawn to Mr. Cancer for there are certain aspects of his character that greatly attract her. His tendency to worship the woman with whom he is involved supplies plenty of fuel for her over-demanding ego. After a period of time, however, his romantic declarations of love could make her feel embarrassed and lose a little of her respect for him. This could be fatal, for above all else Ms. Leo needs to respect her man. This man often has a close bond with his family and relatives, and the generosity in her can tolerate this as long as he does not go to extremes in this direction. The Leo woman is not always conscientious with her housework and he will find fault here, but she does excel as a hostess which will prove useful to him in his chosen career and deepen his affection for her. Invariably, Mr. Cancer takes part in an active sport, possibly connected with water, an activity and an element which hold no interest for her. Although this is a sensitive man, he generally likes to feel that he is the provider in the home, and as Ms. Leo loathes being financially dependent on anybody many arguments will ensue.

A love of alcohol and sport can sometimes combine and deprive Ms. Leo of some of his attention in the bedroom. She may have been looking forward to an early night with him when he arrives home drunk and incapable.

A relationship best avoided.

ARE YOU A TYPICAL LEO MAN?

Answer the questions below, using Yes, No or Sometimes, then turn to page 299 for your answer.

1. Are you accused of taking your woman for granted?

2. Can flattery impair your judgment of character?

3. Can you gracefully accept NO from your date?

4. Are you strongly attracted to the best material things in life?

5. Are you fiercely proud?

6. Do you frown down upon lovemaking in cinemas?

7. Would you complain if your date looked untidy?

8. Is it hard for you to apologize?

9. Sexually would you try anything once just to see what it's like?

10. Do you gamble with life?

11. Are you over-generous with your affection?

12. Does wealth impress you?

13. Do you regard sport as a waste of energy?

14. Do you think that every woman has her price?

15. After a week of sexual abstinence are you bad-tempered?

16. Is it hard for you to sacrifice yourself for others?

17. Do you believe that a man should be the boss in the home?

18. Are you extravagant?

19. Do you forgive easily?

20. Do you think the man should lead in bed?

Total up your score, allowing three for each Yes, two for each Sometimes and one for every No, then turn to page 299.

ARE YOU A TYPICAL LEO WOMAN?

Answer honestly the questions given below, using Yes, No or Sometimes, then turn to page 300 for your answer.

1. Does the idea of back-of-the-car sex appall you?

2. Are you impressed by the appearance of wealth?

3. Do you need regular sex?

4. If your man arrives looking like an unmade bed to take you to the cinema are you annoyed?

5. When sexually frustrated are you likely to go to bed with someone who would not normally attract you?

6. Do you value and look after your possessions?

7. Do you write to someone when it isn't your turn?

8. Does dancing appeal to you?

9. Can pride make it difficult for you to apologize when in the wrong?

10. Are you too often fooled by appearances?

11. Are you a fool for flattery?

12. Do you always put make-up on before going out to the shops?

13. Do you long secretly for a life of ease?

14. Do you hate cheap clothes?

15. Would you feel justified in dropping your boyfriend if he didn't quite come up to your standard in bed?

16. Are you a gambler?

17. Are you attracted to traditional furniture rather than contemporary?

18. Can you forgive and forget?

19. Do you feel a good argument clears the air?

20. Does the idea of a rich husband appeal as long as you could have a good lover discreetly?

Total up your score, allowing three for a Yes, two for a Sometimes and one for a No, then turn to page 300.

VIRGO

THE VIRGIN

The Sign of the Craftsman or Critic

August 24th to September 23rd

THE SECOND EARTH SIGN: *Exact, methodical, industrious, discriminating, intelligent, chaste*

RULER: *Mercury*　　GEMS: *Pink jasper, hyacinth*

COLOR: *Grey or navy blue*　　METAL: *Quicksilver*

Characteristics of the Higher Male

The Virgo individual's chief asset is a splendid power of discrimination. Everything is analyzed, sifted or classified, and this characteristic serves well in his chosen profession for he recognizes at a glance the potential value of others and puts them to work accordingly. Accuracy and method are very important and his careful way with finance can lead to success in the position of banker, accountant or in any occupation where a keen eye for monetary affairs is needed. It is unlikely, however, that he will ever advance far in a situation where authority is concerned for this would entail issuing commands, and when this type attempts to order others around he often gives unintentional offense. Many Virgo men are found in the background of things, usually working harder than any of their colleagues. He applies himself efficiently but quietly, taking in even the smallest details. It is, sadly, quite normal for him to be passed over when praise and appreciation are handed out, for his more extrovert partners may take the credit due to him: in fact, he may appear forever doomed to work without sufficient reward or recognition. Mr. Virgo gives freely of his time and energy but nevertheless there is a limit to his generosity, he senses when demands are excessive and then he will know exactly how to say no and stick to it.

This type is rarely lavish with affection or praise and the wary eye that he keeps on expenditure originates from a fear of dependence on others. Because of this, he lives simply and frugally, and even though extreme wealth may be his he will still continue to spend wisely and carefully.

Love never comes easily to this man, it takes much to melt his heart, but once committed he revels in devoting himself faithfully and loyally to his partner. Neither the male nor female of this sign is over-fond of children, but once they arrive their every need is satisfied, for the Virgo parent wishes to be as perfect in this direction as in all others.

Many of his friends will find him too pure and reticent in discussing his sex life or problems with them. His family and loved ones may maintain that this man is hard to live with and they could be correct: his tendency to play the critic, plus the tight reign he keeps on finances, will not make for an easy life. His standards are high morally and in every other way, and unfortunately—and perhaps unfairly—he expects others to live up to the rules he makes and lives by himself.

He has a strong desire to devote himself to serving others but this does not make him a sexual animal. His partner will need to be a kind and understanding woman, for often he will be thought cold and sexless. Although this is not necessarily true, sex does not occupy a high position on his list and it is difficult for him to express his love verbally. Rather, his love reveals itself in his day-to-day small, thoughtful actions, his presence of mind in a crisis and in the loving care given when loved ones are ill. No other type can so efficiently tend and care for others as the Virgo male or female.

Characteristics of the Higher Female

This woman usually displays a skill of handicraft, finding a use for the most unlikely things, and she is generally considered to be quite ingenious. Her dress sense leans towards a good but simple style often verging on the puritanical. She is intelligent and critical of others, including herself. This is no domestic animal, for her career is important and useful. To spend each day in a purely domestic role would prove detrimental and uncongenial to her, and although her children will be well loved and cared for they will not be her entire life or existence, she needs more to stimulate her intelligence. The desire to serve and tend others leads many of this type into the medical profession.

This woman's more adaptable friends may call her a prude for she has high standards and may appear to others narrow-minded and very fixed in what she believes to be right or wrong sexually.

Characteristics of the Lower Type

This person will be impossible to please, he rarely advances in any field of activity as his eye can inevitably find all the flaws and impossibilities but rarely the possibilities or opportunities in a venture, and although he may destroy ideas and situations he cannot offer suitable alternatives. Because of this tendency, failure is a regular companion of his. He tends to blame prevailing circumstances for his downfall rather than accept that it is he himself who is at fault.

Friends need to be pretty resilient to put up with him, his effect on them can too often be one of depression. Sexually, he finds difficulty in recognizing or accepting anyone as being good enough for him, his critical eye destroying passion before it has had a chance to flower. When badly perverted he becomes masochistic.

Physical Characteristics

A wiry build is associated with this sign and he is usually strong and capable of enduring long hours of work and physical fatigue. Often, the features are irregular and dependent for their beauty on their expression. The eyes are bright and intelligent, the nose heavy. It is common for the female Virgo to be a late developer.

In health this is a very strong sign, illness when it occurs is brought on mostly by overwork and too much absorption in practical matters. Serious illness is rare for he exercises regularly and is fastidious and fussy with his food, taking great care over its preparation.

VIRGO MALE

	Sex	Love	Marriage	Business	Friends (opposite sex)	Friends (same sex)
ARIES						
TAURUS	•	•	•	•	•	•
GEMINI				•		
CANCER	•			•		•
LEO	•					
VIRGO	•			•	•	
LIBRA						
SCORPIO				•		
SAGITTARIUS						
CAPRICORN	•	•	•	•	•	•
AQUARIUS						•
PISCES	•				•	

VIRGO FEMALE

	Sex	Love	Marriage	Business	Friends (opposite sex)	Friends (same sex)
ARIES						
TAURUS	•	•	•	•	•	•
GEMINI				•	•	
CANCER				•		•
LEO						
VIRGO	•			•	•	
LIBRA	•			•		
SCORPIO	•					
SAGITTARIUS						
CAPRICORN	•	•	•	•	•	•
AQUARIUS	•					•
PISCES						

VIRGO MAN tends to have a wiry frame with bony shoulders and thin fingers; fine, often thinning hair; a long nose with a receding chin; bright eyes.

VIRGO WOMAN tends to have a thin body with slim legs and small feet; square shoulders; a long head with almond-shaped eyes, a long nose and a wide mouth.

THE VIRGO PARTNERSHIPS

Virgo Woman with Virgo Man

A mutual outlook on life could be the reason for this relationship starting up, and as both are idealistic it could mean that they will work very hard at it. Attitudes to money are shared, both are ruled by common sense, practicality and a need to save for unforeseen expenses. As long as both Virgos have separate careers then all may be well, but both possess a critical eye which will be turned onto one another, and the less time they have to think about each other's faults the better. Everything participated in, from the cooking of their food to the writing of the laundry list, is executed in laborious detail. It is impossible for a Virgo to be slap-dash. Outside interests need to be encouraged, for these two perfectionists have a lot to offer the world. Physical fitness could preoccupy both and an outdoor activity such as camping or hiking could appeal. Although for the most part very realistic, they can lack a certain sense of proportion and give undue emphasis to small details.

Sexually, they could initially be strongly attracted,

but if one or the other makes a mistake in bed then no hesitation is considered before making a cruel criticism. Sex is unlikely to be the basis of this relationship, however, as too much time will be spent improving matters elsewhere, and in general a warm and affectionate bond should exist.

A nerve-racking relationship.

Virgo Woman with Libra Man

Mr. Libra seems such a charming, sociable and romantic figure—everything, in fact, Ms. Virgo would secretly like to be. When he showers her with compliments and sweeps her off her feet, she will not realize that it is probably the twentieth time this year he has said these things to a woman. She may prefer at first to keep her illusions intact but eventually she will have to face the fact that Mr. Libra can be quite superficial, and this will be the turning point in their relationship. She can either accept him for what he is, a lovable character incapable of fidelity, or run true to form and become bitter and disillusioned. If she carries her dissection of his personality too far she will offend Mr. Libra's keen sense of justice and he will be lost to her. His insistence on being continually involved in fights for the more vulnerable finds little sympathy with Ms. Virgo, for while he is ruled by his feelings she is ruled by her intelligence. She could also be frustrated by his refusal to argue with her; he is likely to call her petty-minded and insensitive, and will refuse to discuss the matter any further. If they are to find any satisfaction together he will have to try to adopt a more realistic attitude to life and she will need to refrain from nagging.

The Libran has many sides to his sexual personality —one day he may try to make love to her while she is doing the ironing, the next he will want to court her for two or three hours before making his first move. The Virgo woman, who is far more straightforward, could regard this as completely unnecessary. If she tells him this, he will not argue but will look around for a more receptive partner.

A relationship which could bring unhappiness to both parties.

Virgo Woman with Scorpio Man

Although two very different people, there is one trait common to both. Each partner here is a born critic with no inhibitions about expressing dissatisfaction, and although both are happy to air their grievances neither is comfortable when the victim of someone else's complaints. When this happens, Ms. Virgo will resort to nagging but Mr. Scorpio will withdraw and seethe with resentment. The complex nature of this man, with his intense likes and dislikes and his emotional insecurity, is difficult for her to understand. Even if she proves herself to be a devoted lover, he will still be consumed with jealousy for no apparent reason. His clear-cut views are also hard for her to take, for she can always see the other person's point of view in an argument while he is totally incapable of doing so. He may arrive at her door expecting sympathy over some injustice he has experienced and will be annoyed when she tries to show him that maybe there was a reason for this. Agreement is generally reached on the financial side of things, for each will respect the other's sensible attitude towards money.

Self-expression is difficult for Mr. Scorpio, and his only form of release seems to be in the bedroom, but when insecure he can be over-demanding. This is basically a cool woman, and the passion and emotion he is capable of showing at these times could be badly handled by her through lack of understanding.

A very difficult relationship.

Virgo Woman with Sagittarius Man

The Sagittarian good humor, outspokenness and liveliness may all appeal to Ms. Virgo, but although she is not jealous by nature Mr. Sagittarius could be the man to arouse these feelings in her. She prefers to be the only woman in her man's life, while he does not believe that love means possession. Where financial security is important to her, he cannot be bothered to spend his time worrying over tomorrow's bills or something that may never happen. Because of this attitude, he is able to chase the most impossible dreams, and because of his good luck they sometimes pay off. Although happy with his good fortune on these occasions, she may resent it a little for she probably works long and hard for little financial reward.

Interest in an outside activity may bring them temporarily together, and a love of travel may be shared, but

these are small things on which to base a relationship.
She could find herself spending many lonely evenings,
due to his probable interest in playing cards or billiards
with the boys. She might even end up encouraging him
in this, for when not preoccupied with these activities
he could quite easily be out chasing some other attractive female.

In general, Ms. Virgo does not place a great emphasis on physical appetites, but Mr. Sagittarius could well
awaken the more basic side of her character as he is
usually a seasoned lover. But the problem of other
women will still exist, and she must either accept this or
forget him.

Not a good union.

Virgo Woman with Capricorn Man

A strong physical attraction could exist between these
two, and similar attitudes to financial matters could
deepen the bond. Ambitious Mr. Capricorn could go
far with the Virgo woman behind him as she understands that his career is all-important to both of them,
and anything she can do to improve his position is willingly tackled. Ms. Virgo's moods are changeable,
however, and when he sinks into one of his black depressions which may last for days she will think he
should be able to shake it off. Nagging should be
avoided at all costs for this can be relied upon to
worsen his state of mind. He may even become self-
destructive, and in order to escape these morbid
thoughts he may take off for a couple of days until he

feels able to cope with life again. It is possible for her to sense the beginnings of this mood and to offer consolation and love before it takes hold of him. The main cause for friction may arise from the Capricorn's tendency to snobbery; he may make friends simply because he is impressed by their wealth or position, and this will meet with disdain and disapproval from Ms. Virgo.

They are a well-matched pair sexually, for neither revolve their world around this side of life, but the experience should be a close and meaningful expression of love, strengthening and not ruling their relationship. His depressions could possibly improve their sexual relations as he will be more vulnerable and therefore more adaptable to her desires.

A good union.

Virgo Woman with Aquarius Man

Initially, Ms. Virgo may be attracted to the activity surrounding this man, his involvement in life will seem exciting to her. And her independent and efficient manner may lead him to heave a sigh of relief at having found a woman who, he believes, will not lean too heavily on him. After a short time, however, their many basic differences will begin to show. Each partner is motivated by mental stimulation, but where she expects to get hers within their relationship by sharing interests and by good conversation, his will be supplied by outside activities. And when on occasions she is looking forward to a cozy evening à deux, he is quite likely to come rushing in preoccupied with some friend's problem and rush out again without giving her a thought. The first or second time this occurs she may be able to stifle her disappointment, but once she realizes that this is the pattern of things to come she is bound to object. The Virgo woman is endowed with a sharp tongue and with Mr. Aquarius she could be in danger of deteriorating into a nagging shrew.

Most Aquarians think there is something sordid about money, while she is very much aware of the ways and means of life, and so monetary affairs will be left to her to juggle with.

There is little likelihood of these two individuals having an easy relationship, and for most of the time happiness could depend on the Virgo's ability to give, as she will be more adaptable than her fixed, and somewhat opinionated, partner.

Their sexual appetites are about equal, but here again outside influences could be the cause of disaster. Ms. Virgo will often have a hard time of it trying to get her Mr. Aquarius' mind off the problems of the world and onto their own sex life, and she will probably find herself having to resort to all the feminine wiles she possesses to keep him from rushing off into the night on a mercy dash for a friend just as they are about to go to bed. This is of course a lot to go through every time she feels like making love, and the consequences will depend on how deeply she loves him; either way, it's going to be tough.

A relationship which is unlikely to develop any further than a short affair.

Virgo Woman with Pisces Man

A man as perceptive as Mr. Pisces can sense every change in Ms. Virgo's moods and emotional needs. He can, of course, also detect the cold and critical side to her, but as he is unlikely to be attracted to these characteristics he may well close his eyes to them. Any decisions that need taking will be left to her, and he will accept her judgement unless she makes a mistake, when he will be quick to draw her attention to it. Financially, once more she will have to take the lead as money seems to burn a hole in Mr. Pisces' pocket, and though he may try to be more practical he will never quite make it. Ms. Virgo likes to discuss sensibly any differences of opinion they may have, but Mr. Pisces will retreat into himself, meditate and try to sort it out on his own, only informing her of his conclusions when they are straight in his mind. This is a relationship where sharing will be difficult. Normally quite cool emotionally, Ms. Virgo may find herself consumed with maternal instincts when he is dejected and forlorn or when life is being particularly hard on him.

Sexually, Mr. Pisces' imagination can run riot, he may talk or think about what she may consider to be outrageous perversions. Trying to go along with him or contribute anything herself could prove a strain on her as the Virgo imagination is somewhat limited.

Concessions are needed to make a success of this relationship.

Virgo Woman with Aries Man

The Virgo and Aries personalities are opposite in many ways, each viewing life from a completely different standpoint. He generally prefers to live in the present; she invariably has one eye firmly on the future. He therefore does not waste time worrying about his financial prospects, always assuming that something will turn up, while the Virgo woman cannot help but plan and worry. Each could think the other totally unreasonable on this point. Ms. Virgo's thoughts of security usually attract her to the type of job which can offer this, in which she will work hard and conscientiously, while Mr. Aries will only work industriously when his job fires his imagination, and this tends to lead to a chequered career. In an attempt to make him see sense— her sense—she could resort to nagging, but sharp words will only inspire amusement in this man, unless he should find himself the continual target for her frustration, and then he is quite likely to move on to a more adaptable partner.

There are also differences in their emotional make- up, for she finds it difficult to fall in love where the impulsive Arietian's feelings are more intense and shorter-lived. As this woman cannot change her own personality and she cannot reasonably expect him to change his, she must accept all of their differences and attempt to keep complaints to herself instead of airing them at the first opportunity.

Sexually, his appetites once more vary where hers are

pretty constant. Her masochistic tendencies may have been the reason for this attraction in the first place; should he sense this, she might arouse his more sadistic side. In all fairness, Ms. Virgo would need to be a saint to successfully accept and live with this man; she could save herself much frustration if she were to pass him by or run fast when he approaches.

A disastrous union.

Virgo Woman with Taurus Man

The Taurean man is friendly, patient and honest with his feelings, far more on her wavelength than the previous character. Their outlook on life and attitudes to finance are identical. Both enjoy planning the future down to the last detail, and they share a deep-rooted fear of debt, providing a good basis on which to build a solid relationship. Mr. Taurus enjoys his home and all the comforts it can offer, and although the Virgo woman may not be mad about housework the home is always efficiently run and his needs always catered for. Emotionally, the Taurean is the more intense of the two, but it is possible that in time he may provoke more intensity in Ms. Virgo. His jealousy could cause some tension from time to time but this woman will give him little cause for real anxiety, and this streak in his personality will make her feel secure. One cause for friction could be his tendency towards laziness, which cannot fail to offend this hard-working woman. These phases of his normally pass fairly quickly, however, and she would be well-advised to simply ignore them.

Another danger exists with this combination of characters: their conservative attitudes and love of the domestic environment may lead to a cutting-off of the outside world, and while they may enjoy each other's company this could eventually lead to staleness and boredom. When the relationship appears to be drifting into this state, they should make a real effort to participate in a more active social life.

They will have a very active sexual life but it is likely to be conservative and straightforward, although she is intelligent enough to go along with any suggestions he may make. Each partner is likely to live for each other. An ideal union.

Virgo Woman with Gemini Man

A long relationship between these signs would be rare, but it could happen that the Virgo woman in her late twenties be partly maternally attracted to this childish man. His versatility, search for communication, and charm are regarded by her as immature and she may be inclined to patronize him, deciding that in time he will outgrow these tendencies. Later she will realize that restlessness is part of his character, and then she may decide to try to change him, but although this man needs a steadying influence in his life it must be provided unobtrusively, for if aware of it he will try to prove that he does not need it.

Clashes are also bound to occur between her love of routine and his preference for chaos; her well-run orderly life could make him feel restricted and possessed, and could eventually drive him away. Mr. Gemini is stimulated by challenge, but if their problems seem to be smoothing out he will lose interest. Ms. Virgo on the other hand prefers to persevere in her relationships. It may be possible for them to reach some kind of agreement if she appeals to his intelligence, for the only thing they have in common is an over-active mind that likes to be exercised daily.

Sexually, this man may have an unfortunate influence on her, for she is rarely versatile in this field and friction outside the bedroom can make it difficult for her to give herself to him at all, while he needs a woman who will listen to any suggestions he may make and one who can supply novelty and excitement. It is almost certain that within a short period of time he will search for this elsewhere, leaving her angry and frustrated.

Not a good relationship.

Virgo Woman with Cancer Man

The Cancer man, who is ruled by his emotions and who remains a romantic always, will find life difficult with a woman such as Ms. Virgo, who is ruled by common sense and intelligence. She may find his emotional intensity frightening, for she cannot understand his constant need for reassurance and love—she feels this should be unnecessary. When denied this expression of devotion, he may assume a martyr complex or sulk unendingly, and instead of offering him some consolation Ms. Virgo will appeal to his common sense and logic, which are non-existent in him in this frame of mind. Such sensitiv-

ity she could find intolerable in time and she may lose
respect for him as a man and possibly look around for
someone a little stronger. Further battles may rage over
his involvement with his parents, brothers, sisters *et al,*
for this is basically a family man at heart. Ms. Virgo is
much more detached. There are, however, two things in
their favor: they are both shrewd in financial matters,
and they both love home-life. And there is, of course,
always the possibility of her growing less down-to-earth
under his influence, in which case their chances of happiness will be greatly increased.

Sexually, however, once more the over-sensitivity of
the Cancerian could create problems. His persistently
romantic and loving approach could conflict when she
is feeling more basic, and he is likely to consider her
cold and unfeeling.

A relationship which needs a lot of hard work.

Virgo Woman with Leo Man

If given time to think, Ms. Virgo is unlikely to be attracted to this man, but with his overpowering personality and generosity with himself she may be swept into
a wild infatuation and not realize their basic incompatibility until she has cooled down. His deep need for
flattery and admiration cannot be fulfilled within this
relationship as compliments are hard for her to express,
and when his ego begins to crumble he could become
arrogant and overbearing. Conflict once more arises
through financial matters, as his extravagance and generosity can be relied upon to aggravate the mean side of

her character, forcing her into adopting a stubborn, miserly attitude. The more he spends, the meaner she will become, and many fights will ensue.

Although deeply engrossed in his career sometimes, these periods are invariably followed by phases of sheer laziness—something totally incomprehensible to the Virgoan. Her nagging on this point will have little effect. There is, however, a chance that his warmth may penetrate her cold fury and in time she may yield on some of these sore points, but it would be foolhardy to rely on this occurring.

While he still sees her as a feminine, attractive woman he will be passionate and loving, but once he starts thinking of her as cold and nagging he will lose interest, find her unattractive, and start looking elsewhere.

This is unlikely to be a harmonious relationship.

ARE YOU A TYPICAL VIRGO MAN?

Answer the questions given below, using Yes, No or Sometimes, then turn to page 301 for your answer.

1. Do you feel unappreciated at work?

2. Do you take any physical exercise to keep yourself fit?

3. Do you admire men like James Bond?

4. Do you prefer your sexual affairs one at a time?

5. Are you critical?

6. Do you think that routine is important?

7. Are you fussy with your food?

8. Do you long to be more extrovert in bed?

9. Do you take time over everything you do?

10. Can you be faithful in a lengthy relationship?

11. Do homosexuals embarrass you?

12. Are you shocked by other people's sexual habits and behavior?

13. Would being in debt worry you?

14. Are you turned-off easily over some small thing?

15. Would you notice if your woman was wearing a new sweater?

16. Do you lose respect for women whose sexual appetites can equal men's?

17. Are you conscientious?

18. Do you think that families should be limited to two children?

19. Do you always make certain that someone has taken precautions before making love?

20. Can you do without much sleep?

Total up your score allowing three for a Yes, two for a Sometimes and one for a No, then turn to page 301.

ARE YOU A TYPICAL VIRGO WOMAN?

Answer honestly the questions listed below using Yes, No and Sometimes, then turn to page 302 for your answer.

1. Do you think the importance of motherhood is overemphasized?

2. Are you fussy about your food?

3. Do you think that financial security is more important than sex in marriage?

4. Would dirty finger-nails put you off making love to the owner?

5. Are you critical?

6. Is it hard for you to make new suggestions in bed?

7. Do you think that others may consider your sexual morals old-fashioned?

8. Can you abstain from sex for a week with ease?

9. Are you happy to be financially independent of your man?

10. Do you enjoy looking after others?

11. Would you be horrified if your unmarried daughter became pregnant?

12. Do you believe in method and order?

13. Does your taste in clothing center on simplicity?

14. Can you work hard on little sleep?

15. Does waste of any description worry you?

16. Would you make an excuse if you were not feeling like sex and your man was feeling amorous?

17. Do you think that permissiveness has gone too far?

18. Do you have neat handwriting?

19. Does your mind work quickly?

20. Do you think that men have an easier life?

Total up your score allowing three for a Yes, two for a Sometimes and one for a No, then turn to page 302.

LIBRA

THE SCALES

The Sign of the Statesman or Manager

September 24th to October 23rd

THE SECOND AIR SIGN: *Restless, versatile, exuberant, intelligent, artistic, talkative*

RULER: *Venus*   **GEMS:** *Diamond, opal*

COLOR: *Indigo blue*   **METAL:** *Copper*

Characteristics of the Higher Male

The Libran man is noted for his keen sense of justice and fairness which when offended is championed with formidable energy. All that is truly beautiful around him is appreciated, admired and delighted in, ugliness in any form is despised. Dishonesty, melancholia, hysteria are all abhorred and escaped from at the first opportunity. He goes through life attempting to establish a beautiful and harmonious environment for those with whom he comes into contact. He labors in vigorous phases followed by periods of complete relaxation, during which time he may isolate himself from the outside world while he recuperates. Once back on his feet he resumes the previous hectic pace. Such behavior is quite normal for him, and when successful in life it is generally as some kind of specialist. As a friend, this man is in great demand as his charm, courtesy and genuine appreciation of what is good in others make both male and female find him an illuminating companion. At the onset, his vocation or career may cause some anxiety for he may make a wrong decision or take a wrong turning, but in time his particular talents will reveal themselves and will frequently lead him into an artistic activity.

Love is of paramount importance in his life, even in old age he rarely loses interest. The real danger to him is his urge to propose to the first attractive female that happens his way, living in many instances to regret it. With luck his refinement and fastidious tastes may save him, but should he fall into such a snare and then awaken abruptly to his foolishness, he may launch into many affairs in search for what is missing from his life, normally bringing much unhappiness upon himself and others.

Children are attracted to this man, they sense the fun that radiates from him and he is usually ready to respond to them, provided they can refrain from imposing on his kind nature too much.

Sex plays an important part in his life though it is the love of chase and challenge that really stimulates. Mr. Libra begins early in his pursuit of the opposite sex. Any female who takes him on on a permanent basis will be forever busy controlling his wandering eye and she will need to be glamorous and imaginative at all times or his interest may soon begin to fade.

Characteristics of the Higher Female

Although sister Libran runs the same risks as her brother, she also shares the same protections and her uncritical mind and frank admiration for the male generally lead to popularity with the opposite sex. The chief source of trouble seems to be her manner of appearing too obliging, for she finds it difficult to hurt another's feelings and the word NO comes too infrequently to avoid problems and stress. This female attracts complications and is puzzled as to the reason, although it will usually lie in her mistaken kindliness.

Ms. Libra makes an excellent wife and one whose entire world will revolve around her man, and often this is taken to such a degree that her children may play a poor second fiddle. The maternal instinct is not to the fore of her personality and she will always put the man in her life before all else, for she discovered at an early age that self-sufficiency is not for her, as only with the man she loves can she find true expression.

Characteristics of the Lower Type

The lower Libran is a jack-of-all-trades and his parents may despair over his start in life but to no avail, for he tries this and that, rarely making a success of anything attempted. Believing himself to be on the search for perfection, he splits hairs and potters over work, his indecision painful to those around. This type has a short memory in affections and it is impossible for him or her to suffer from a broken heart for very long, despite protestations to the contrary.

To be easily pleased and to please easily, to be born attractive with a need for all that is fair and lovely in life, and to possess a hatred for ugly, unharmonious and mean fellow creatures can be sufficient reason for an impossible life, but add to this an inclination to always live in the present and for the present, caring little for what hides in the future or what has hurt in the past, and you have an individual with a burden to carry. Because of these tendencies this type will bring misfortune to himself and all those who enter into his life, still protesting his innocence after each unhappy incident.

Physical Characteristics

The true Libran has a heart-shaped mouth, a dimple in his chin, and generally appears to look happy. He seems well-fed and is prone to plumpness, dimples, curves and rounded contours, but not necessarily to excessive fat.

A sweet voice, a bright ringing laugh and an appreciation of fun in those around are all usually in evidence. Fair skin and hair are associated with this sign.

In health this type is strong as long as his sense of balance remains undisturbed, but when upset the nerves and constitution will suffer indirectly. If rundown he should rest, watch his diet and develop his appreciative qualities through poetry, music or some art form.

LIBRA MALE

	Sex	Love	Marriage	Business	Friends (opposite sex)	Friends (same sex)
ARIES	•				•	
TAURUS				•	•	•
GEMINI	•	•	•		•	•
CANCER	•					
LEO					•	
VIRGO	•			•		
LIBRA	•			•	•	•
SCORPIO						
SAGITTARIUS	•					
CAPRICORN						
AQUARIUS		•	•	•		•
PISCES					•	•

LIBRA FEMALE

	Sex	Love	Marriage	Business	Friends (opposite sex)	Friends (same sex)
ARIES	•				•	
TAURUS	•					•
GEMINI		•	•	•	•	•
CANCER	•				•	
LEO	•					•
VIRGO						
LIBRA	•			•	•	•
SCORPIO						
SAGITTARIUS	•					
CAPRICORN						
AQUARIUS		•	•	•		•
PISCES					•	•

LIBRA MAN tends to have a rounded, curvy frame with thin arms and pronounced hips and thighs; a short neck; a square face with a cupid's-bow mouth and possibly some dimples.

LIBRA WOMAN tends to have a medium-build, curvy body with a large bust and good legs; light-colored hair; a square jaw; pale eyes and a heart-shaped mouth with dimples.

THE LIBRA PARTNERSHIPS

Libra Woman with Libra Man

This relationship promises to be quite an exhausting one, for both partners tend to be bursting with vitality and over-demanding with those they love. Neither will want to spend too much time in the home, they need plenty of outside interests to keep them happy—if these are denied them, frustration and neurotic tendencies may set in. Each has a well-developed sense of justice, bringing to their home many fights for their more vulnerable friends and acquaintances. Animals may stray willy-nilly into their flat, for neither can bear to see an ill-treated or starving creature.

Each understands that the partnership needs hard work and understanding, and much effort will go into theirs to make it as harmonious as possible. Librans are generally avid lovers of beauty; some artistic interest may be shared, or they may put great effort into making their home as beautiful as possible, for members of this sign are hypersensitive to environment and need to retreat at times from the exertions of their outside interests. Life promises to be hectic, and they will rarely be alone for friends will feel perfectly free to drop in at any old time, knowing they will always be welcome.

Sexually, the attraction between them could be overpowering, and each may make a real effort to think up ways of pleasing the other. The relationship could be threatened by a third party, however, as both are strongly attracted to the opposite sex—but they could well have the kind of agreement where infidelity is taken in its stride. Mr. and Ms. Libra need plenty of excitement, and they should find it within this union.

A good relationship, but one that is unfortunately unlikely to last.

Libra Woman with Scorpio Man

The Libra woman could be flattered and fascinated by Mr. Scorpio's intense declarations of love. Initially, his possessiveness and jealousy may seem attractive, but after a while she will begin to feel hemmed in and try to pull away. Immediately when this happens, he will cling on tighter and attempt to restrict all of her movements. If this should result in driving her into an affair with somebody else, she should not expect this man to forgive and forget; if he does take her back, it may well be for reasons of revenge, simply wanting to make her life a misery for a while, and if the Libran is of the lower type she could find it very difficult to stand up to him. In this relationship, her sense of justice is bound to be offended for the Scorpio man has keen likes and dislikes, and when she tries to question these he will not be able to explain his feelings.

In order to achieve some harmony she must recognize the genuine and deep love he has for her and try to be a little more considerate while he must do his best to open up his mind as much as possible. If Mr. Scorpio wants to have peace of mind with this woman, he will have to take care of the financial side of life himself, as Ms. Libra cannot see the need to worry or budget.

Each possesses a keen sexual appetite, but while he is all passion and emotion, she needs mental stimulation and excitement if she is to remain with one man for long. Her need for sex is invariably triggered by the frame of mind she is in at the time. This can be influenced by a film she may have seen, a book she may have read, or some small thing mentioned during the day. It is up to him to discover what turns her on, and use it accordingly.

This union is likely to belong to the love/hate variety, for middle-of-the-road compromise will not satisfy either.

Libra Woman with Sagittarius Man

Ms. Libra and Mr. Sagittarius may meet at half past seven one evening and be in bed together at eight o'clock, for inhibition is not part of either personality. The gay, feminine and pleasure-loving Libran will be very attracted to this frank, broadminded and happy-go-lucky man. Their relationship is also likely to be based on friendship, as each believes this to be essential to any love affair. When he comes to her with some mad inspiration, however impractical it may be she will always offer her encouragement and good wishes, and if the whole scheme collapses she will be unconcerned about the repercussions, her first thought will be for him.

The Sagittarian man may frequently boast that he does not have a jealous bone in his body, but to his great disbelief he may find himself experiencing this emotion with Ms. Libra, as she is often the popular type who is always surrounded by clamoring admirers at parties and gatherings. Finances could be chaotic in this union for neither has a practical head when it comes to handling money; one of them must try to develop a little common sense here or pressure from the outside could disturb their happiness.

Although this relationship may seem perfect, the strong attraction between them is unlikely to last; each prefers a life in constant motion. But while together, this could be something neither of them will ever forget. Their sex life is likely to be very special, he loves to flatter, court and romance her and Ms. Libra can listen all night as this is exactly what she needs to stimulate her sexual appetite.

This is likely to be a wild infatuation rather than a more meaningful relationship.

Libra Woman with Capricorn Man

On the rebound from some mad affair, Mr. Capricorn's organized life may appeal to Ms. Libra. But later, when she realizes that she is no longer free to do her own impulsive thing, she is likely to be somewhat disenchanted. For a while, however, she will be happy to play hostess to the guests he entertains in order to further his career, and he will be delighted by her ability in this direction. In money matters, life could be difficult. He worries, plans, and is likely to save everything he can rather zealously; the easy-come, easy-go Libran finds this behavior obsessive and unreasonable, and will tell him so before long. Agreement here can never be reached. Also, the Capricorn's attitude to work could eventually produce problems, for although she can respect a man engrossed in his career she expects him to be able to switch this off rather more than he is capable of doing. Ms. Libra will expect verbal assurances of undying love, and while she may be patient with him at first, believing that this will come later, eventually she will accuse him of being cold and unfeeling.

The tension between them is likely to be increased by their sex life, as his career keeps his mind busy and therefore off her. In an attempt to attract his attention she will resort to feminine wiles, and he is unlikely to understand what is happening. A female such as Ms. Libra cannot be expected to stay around this man too long, she will be on her way practicing her gifts on a more receptive audience.

An unwise relationship.

Libra Woman with Aquarius Man

These two could well meet in the midst of their social whirl and from then on they will have great difficulty in finding any time to be alone together, for they are both attracted to activity, excitement and unusual people. She will quite understand when the phone rings at three in the morning and he feels the necessity to rush off into the night to aid some friend—she may even go with him; and should he arrive home with some strange-looking person he has taken pity on she will be the first to make the intruder feel at home. There are certain aspects of each personality which cannot agree, but it will usually be possible to reach a compromise. While she may be hurt by some cruel remark made by a friend, he finds this difficult to understand as the opinions of others do not mean much to him, and although he may be sympathetic he is certain to believe that she has over-reacted. The biggest problem in their relationship could be her sentimental streak clashing with his logic—this can take many forms, but on each occasion she will be left nursing bruised feelings while he will be confused.

Up to this point, sex may not have meant much to the Aquarian man, but this might be just the girl to change all this; she is an impulsive lover, and although amused by this at first he could learn to appreciate the value of spontaneity. She may also show him how to use his active brain in this side of their relationship by revealing to him the difference a little imagination can make to sex.

A stimulating relationship.

Libra Woman with Pisces Man

Ms. Libra could meet Mr. Pisces while on one of her errands of mercy, for Mr. Pisces invariably believes that somebody somewhere is doing him an injustice. On getting to know him better, she will approve of his sensitivity, romantic inclinations and ability to make her feel the most beautiful woman in the world. It can only be a short time, however, before she also experiences his deep depressions, and she may consider at this point that he takes life far too seriously, for where she play-acts most of the time he generally feels deeply. Her method of offering consolation must be carefully thought out, for it is too easy for her to appear patronizing and this will irritate him and could result in a neurotic burst of temper. There may be times when she will wonder if he has ever had a sense of humor and she could tease him playfully about this, only to be confronted with an aggressive retort.

In any relationship a Piscean man can be secretive, but with a Libran who constantly tries to analyze his every thought he could withdraw even more than he would normally, trying to find some peace and quiet. She will not understand this and many heated arguments will ensue, and her lack of constancy may lead her eventually to give up and search for a less complex partner. If she wants a harmonious existence she will have to put this man before her own desires—something she finds most difficult to do.

Their sex life should work out fine provided she can control her tendency to be over-demanding, for Mr. Pisces prefers to take the lead in bed to prove his strength and masculinity. It would be better for her to allow this, because although she is capable of taking over, if she does the loss will be hers.

A complicated partnership.

Libra Woman with Aries Man

This is an attraction which often occurs but rarely lasts, for basically these are two very different characters. She believes in equality within a relationship and is at first amused by his attempts to dominate, but later her sense of humor will desert her when she realizes that he really expects to be the unchallenged leader. Also, her natural gift for self-expression will automatically be frustrated with a man who largely lives in the head and believes that verbal endearments are a sign of weakness. The initial attraction could be stimulated by their mutually impulsive natures—"it seemed like a good idea at the time." Sentimentality is alien to this man's personality; he refuses to be nostalgic about the past or dream about the future, his thoughts remain firmly in the present, and if she wants to look back over their relationship or make plans for their future he will refuse to co-operate, leaving her with a feeling of insecurity and unimportance.

She will always help and consider others, especially

those in trouble, but the "me first" attitude of the Arietian scorns such behavior, thinking it a waste of time. The Arietian male may occasionally use her inferiority complexes to his own advantage, for he is attracted to helpless women and even though it may make her very unhappy he may sadistically try to keep her down. Her wish to be independent of him he regards as hurtful. This state of affairs is unlikely to last very long for their relationship began on impulse and could easily end the same way.

Sexually, although competent, Mr. Aries can be inhibited, and her attempts to draw him out will be misconstrued as a slight on his masculinity. The other differences in personality are also reflected here—he will hate any attempt of hers to take the lead in love-making—and altogether this relationship should be avoided whenever possible.

Libra Woman with Taurus Man

This relationship could stem from a mutual interest in an artistic pursuit; both are fascinated by beauty and the people who create it. Unfortunately, this is not sufficient in itself to form the basis of a good relationship. The Taurean man basically believes that a woman's place is in the home; while in one of her home-making moods, Ms. Libra could be quite happy with this philosophy, but this frame of mind is unlikely to last and her need for independence will soon begin to show. Once this happens, Mr. Taurus will feel that he is losing her and his stubborn and aggressive side will come to

the surface, but his threats and ravings will fall on deaf
ears. He must accept that he cannot possess the Libran
woman. Jealousy will also provide cause for friction—
he may continually question her about her movements
and suggest that she has been unfaithful. After a while,
he could in fact drive her to this.

Attitudes to money differ considerably, he is plagued
by insecurity and tries to provide for their future while
she can only think of her immediate requirements and
does not always count the cost too carefully.

She will at first be happy with him as a lover, for the
Taurean appetite is good, but eventually she will feel
that he is too conservative and set in his ways to satisfy
her own needs, which will mainly consist of mental
stimulation. She could well rebel and abstain until he is
willing to become more versatile. When it becomes apparent that adaptability is not part of his make-up she
will look around for a more flexible man.

A stormy relationship.

Libra Woman with Gemini Man

A search for novelty and excitement is shared by Ms.
Libra and Mr. Gemini and may be the main factor in
bringing them together. To begin with, they will rush
around in a mad circle enjoying themselves and indulging in activity of all kinds, but this normally impractical
woman may quite suddenly start worrying about his
irresponsible behavior. Finances could also cause her
concern, and it will be left to her to introduce some
stability here. This must, however, be tackled in such a

way that her Geminian will hardly notice her efforts. She could lose some of her appeal with this sudden concern for common sense. In need of a steady influence herself at times, she may resent the fact that it is always she who must accommodate his moods and ideas, although the attraction is likely to be so strong that she will not mind giving in this direction.

He has no special thoughts on career women, and if she is very involved with hers he will offer encouragement and enthusiasm whenever it is needed. If he can cultivate the ability to listen to others their relationship will benefit. Both partners being attracted to travel, they will enjoy many short, spur-of-the-moment trips.

Their sex life will swing, each knows exactly how to excite the other and just living together will provide all the stimulation they need. A third person is unlikely to cause a rift in their relationship, as neither will attach undue importance to infidelity.

An excellent partnership.

Libra Woman with Cancer Man

After a torrid affair with some irresponsible character Mr. Cancer's obvious devotion and strong domestic impulses may appeal to Ms. Libra, but this mood is unlikely to last for it is difficult for her to sustain a particular frame of mind for any length of time. Her strong need for a social circle, an active career, and involvement in life in general will eventually clash with a man who takes his enjoyment at home. The more she tries to coax him out the more stubborn he will become, and later on she will begin to take her pleasures outside while he is left sulking and brooding alone. It may even be difficult for them to argue, for he uses his emotions on these occasions while she uses her head, and so discussion is unlikely to benefit the situation. A temporary closeness may be found when her sentimentality and his romanticism coincide.

Although Mr. Cancer could not be accused of meanness, his common sense will rebel at the money she spends on clothes and accessories; he will not understand that it helps to build her ego and make her feel more feminine, or that this is an important part of her personality. To him it is mere extravagance.

The Cancer man is usually involved in some form of sport—the comradeship appeals to him—while the Libran woman prefers a more sophisticated way of spending her leisure time and will object to standing out in the rain for several hours while he kicks a ball around.

Their sex life will develop into a constant battle of emotion against intellect; Ms. Libra is not a woman who appreciates the soft touch, while he is unlikely to understand her need for mental stimulation.

The relationship may get by if both parties possess sufficient determination, but few people will be capable of making a success of this combination.

Libra Woman with Leo Man

Such a feminine woman as Ms. Libra cannot help but be attracted to the masculinity of Mr. Leo. The vital way he lives his life will appeal strongly to her, although she may be quite shocked when he lapses into a phase of total laziness. It will not take her long, however, to realize that a good dose of flattery will set him in motion again. His need to dominate in their relationship may worry and depress her at first, but with such a warm and generous character it is possible for her to adapt to this. Her sense of justice may be enraged when the Leo man refuses to apologize when he has been wrong—his pride makes this very difficult for him.

As a couple they will be very popular with their guests for nothing is too good for the Leo's friends and the Libran excels as a hostess. Money spent on the finer things of life could render them poverty-stricken in a short time unless common sense is brought to bear on the situation. It may be up to him to become more financially responsible; this could be encouraged by the helpless female act at which she is proficient. Although jealousy is not a strong part of the Leo personality, this may be aroused if her career is more successful than his own, therefore she would be well advised to keep her achievements quietly to herself.

Sexually, he will keep her busy and therefore happy. This aspect of life promises to be a satisfactory one for both and may be the lifesaver in the relationship, for both find it easy to express their love and enjoy pleasing one another in bed. She can give much to someone as warm-hearted as Mr. Leo.

A fiery but good partnership.

Libra Woman with Virgo Man

A stimulating conversation could be the beginning of this attraction. Both partners possessing keen and observant minds, they will analyze their friends, families and the world—but she will feel uncomfortable when his critical eye is turned upon her, dissecting her personality and parading her faults before her. The Libran woman is more active socially than the Virgo; he sometimes finds it difficult to relax and enjoy himself where this comes naturally to her, and he may accuse her of irresponsibility and a flippant attitude towards life. Her way of becoming involved in other people's problems and fights can meet with his approval, until she becomes emotionally involved, when his sympathy evaporates. The expression of love is achieved in very different ways; she must learn to recognize his in the things he does for her rather than in the things he says, and her natural verbal talent may be frustrated and inhibited.

The Virgo man will expect her to account for every penny spent, and if he suspects that she is being extravagant she may have a hard time getting money out of him at all. Her talent for collecting pets of all descriptions is tolerated provided she can keep them under control, for this is a fussy man in all things. When she has spent three hours preparing an exotic meal, a little thing like a cracked dish can take all the pleasure out of it for him.

Sexually, their differences could be impossible to reconcile. To him, sex is a functional activity to be indulged in occasionally, while to her it is a way of life, a full-time preoccupation. Such differing attitudes must lead to trouble and eventually, aided by other problems like money and social life, to someone else's bed.

Not a good union.

ARE YOU A TYPICAL LIBRAN MAN?

Answer honestly the questions given below, using Yes, No or Sometimes, then turn to page 303 for the answer.

1. Are you interested in women's fashion?

2. Is your wandering eye difficult to control?

3. Are you attracted to glamorous women?

4. Do ugly shows of temperament turn you off?

5. Is your work pattern erratic?

6. Does injustice offend you?

7. Do you think you could enjoy a sex orgy?

8. Are you artistic?

9. Do you fall in love easily?

10. Is it hard for you to say NO to those you love?

11. Do you have a complicated life?

12. Do you enjoy playing with children?

13. Are decisions hard for you to make?

14. Have you often thought you were in love with two women at the same time?

15. Is sex a failure for you if your woman is unsatisfied?

16. Do you think you are oversexed?

17. Are you good at expressing inner emotion?

18. Do you think that partnership is a work of art?

19. Would you repeatedly leave jobs where injustice was condoned?

20. Do you believe in sexual equality?

Total up your score allowing three for a Yes, two for a Sometimes and one for a No, then turn to page 303.

ARE YOU A TYPICAL LIBRAN WOMAN?

Answer the questions given below, using Yes, No and Sometimes, then turn to page 304 for the answer.

1. Do you find yourself in difficult situations through your inability to say No?

2. Do you consider yourself to be a feminist?

3. Do you enjoy seducing your men?

4. Do you find violent men repellent?

5. Do you live for the man in your life?

6. Is it hard for you to exist without love?

7. Do you think it is wrong for a woman to be a careerist?

8. Do you like cats?

9. Do you ever dream or think of being in bed with two of your lovers at the same time?

10. Does beauty exalt you?

11. Do you think a man's body can be beautiful?

12. Do you admire glamorous, famous women?

13. Are you capable of deep hatred for men?

14. Do you wear bright colors?

15. Are you guilty of crazy ideas and schemes?

16. Does the thought of motherhood worry you?

17. Are you musical?

18. Are you hurt when criticized?

19. Do you secretly like possessive men?

20. Do you rebel against injustice?

Total up your score, allowing three for a Yes, two for a Sometimes and one for a No, then turn to page 304.

SCORPIO

THE SCORPION

The Sign of the Governor or Inspector

October 24th to November 22nd

THE SECOND WATER SIGN: *Energetic, independent, passionate, determined, with keen likes and dislikes*

RULER: *Mars*   **GEMS:** *Topaz, malachite*

COLOR: *Deep red*   **METAL:** *Steel*

Characteristics of the Higher Male

The male Scorpio is well known for his judgement, he can criticize perfectly and impartially, and he is able to give his verdict in a clear and decisive manner. Attributed with quick thought, Mr. Scorpio can immediately see the purpose and meaning of things which come under his penetrating eye.

The love of power is well-developed but his ambitions are not confined to himself, he desires progress for others also. His perceptions are strong and when his career relies on them to any great extent, a high position is often attained. The Scorpio man can make an excellent doctor, policeman or inspector. The highest achievement is in his ability to use this power in the most difficult of situations. He strives for self-mastery or improvement, but his downfall is frequently brought about by the sting in his personality which is too often aimed at the wrong people at the wrong time.

In love this man tends to be intense and exclusive, prone to sudden attachments and equally sudden separations, this generally stemming from the positive love or hatred felt for his fellow man. It is impossible for him to feel indifferent about anyone or anything. Sentimentality is frowned upon, the Scorpio male loathes gush of any description and although he may attempt to express inner emotion when in love, it does not come without much effort and eventually defeat may be acknowledged in this direction. This man is rarely easily matched but once this step has been taken, his fixed views on loyalty and trust come to the fore. His eagle eye can serve him well here, for it may prevent him from rushing into a hasty marriage or engagement, and despite the fact that many Scorpios can recognize their future wife or husband on sight, nevertheless they will still wait and watch before taking the final plunge.

He can be brusque and abrupt when he wishes, but his self-control is strong and regularly exercised over his intense sexual urge, for the Scorpio male is motivated by a fear that rightly tells him it would be impossible for him to be ruled by his keen passions. No woman will find him an easy person to live with, he can be tiresome and irritating on occasions, trust is rarely totally given for little faith is placed in his fellow man and when betrayed, though it may only be to the slightest degree, he feels justified in these beliefs. Because of such tendencies friends will belong to a tight, close and exclusive circle. Mr. Scorpio could be summarized as determined, reserved, tenacious and secretive, somewhat proud and capable of unmistakable traits of character which cause him to be intensely liked or disliked. His strong backbone, however, helps him to accomplish far more than subjects born of the weaker signs.

Sexually this an active male who is stimulated by passion and emotion, and he needs a female who is sufficiently warm and sensitive to appreciate this.

Characteristics of the Higher Female

Ms. Scorpio does not find it easy when it comes to personal relationships for she is apt to be exacting and hard to live with. Efficient and strong, it is most difficult for her to make allowances for the weaknesses of others, and she is rigidly stern when matters of principle are at stake. Too often this type will become detrimentally involved with a weaker man who will awaken all of her most undesirable characteristics, but she may consider him better than no man at all.

Despite her strength of personality, this is a pure female, passionate, sensual and with a large capacity for love. Generally speaking these good qualities are not wasted on just anyone, only to those who have won her love and respect will she show her softer and more loving side. This subject makes an excellent mother though she tends to expect too much from her offspring, often placing before them almost impossible targets. Jealousy is an inescapable part of her personality and the man she eventually marries will discover that no matter how much reassurance is given, it will never be enough.

Characteristics of the Lower Type

When this individual is bad, he is very bad. Incidents which create mild resentment or dislike in others create in him violent anger, fierce pride, jealousy and hatred. His passions are all-consuming and his courage never fails him, for his will is of iron, but unless he can harness these characteristics he may become a reckless gambler or an insatiable drinker.

It is impossible for this man or woman to take a back seat, and he may resort to unfair or unjust criticism in an effort to attract the attention of others. He is secretly delighted if he should uncover a weaker or more fallible being and usually proceeds to expose his or her faults to those around. Such a man openly enjoys watching friends waste their time and this can lead to a love of practical jokes, which does little to enhance his popularity. These obvious shortcomings find their origins in the Scorpio sting, and this type can unconsciously turn it onto himself and become self-destructive while attempting to destroy others.

Physical Characteristics

This sign endows its subjects with a powerful frame and inclines them towards being thick-set. The eyes are dark and penetrating, the features often heavy. A certain pride is displayed in the command of feature and immobility of expression.

Feelings are rarely shown on the surface even when deeply stirred, and he enjoys turning his perceptions on to others, enabling him to read them as he would an open book. In health there is a tremendous amount of endurance and his powers of recovery are great. A Scorpio subject takes pride in the length of time he can work without sleep and mostly will be lucky enough to get away with it, but when he finally does fall ill, no patient is more trying, for this man will refuse to put his faith in anyone other than himself.

SCORPIO MALE

	Sex	Love	Marriage	Business	Friends (opposite sex)	Friends (same sex)
ARIES						
TAURUS	•					
GEMINI						
CANCER		•	•		•	•
LEO	•					
VIRGO	•					
LIBRA						
SCORPIO	•			•		
SAGITTARIUS						
CAPRICORN				•	•	•
AQUARIUS	•			•		
PISCES		•	•	•	•	•

SCORPIO FEMALE

	Sex	Love	Marriage	Business	Friends (opposite sex)	Friends (same sex)
ARIES						
TAURUS						
GEMINI						
CANCER		•	•	•	•	•
LEO						
VIRGO				•		
LIBRA						
SCORPIO	•			•		
SAGITTARIUS						
CAPRICORN				•	•	•
AQUARIUS	•				•	
PISCES		•	•	•	•	•

SCORPIO MAN tends to have a big, powerful frame with muscular legs and large, square hands; a large head with heavy eyebrows, a big nose, deep-set, penetrating eyes and a strong mouth.

SCORPIO WOMAN tends to have a strong, wiry frame with a slim figure; dark, silky hair; strong, sharp features with well-marked eyebrows, penetrating eyes and small ears.

THE SCORPIO PARTNERSHIPS

Scorpio Woman with Scorpio Man

This attraction could be on impact, and the wild infatuation that follows may later develop into a deep love. Although Scorpios have many virtues their faults can be extreme, but if both of them come to realize and accept their weak spots they will avoid unnecessary tension. Violent likes and dislikes are a typical Scorpio trait, and if these do not coincide each will refuse to budge an inch or admit that he or she is wrong. Suspicion and jealousy are also deeply ingrained in subjects of this sign, but their natural loyalty should be able to keep this under control.

Career problems could create difficulty for Mr. Scorpio must be THE most important influence in their relationship and if he feels his masculinity threatened his aggressive side begins to show. When arguments do take place (and they will) they could be sufficiently violent to deteriorate into physical fights. The inability to forgive and forget can make life intolerable for two

Scorpios together. Where with another woman he may be nagged at for drowning his sorrows in drink, Ms. Scorpio is quite likely to grab a glass and drown hers alongside. No financial problems should arise, however, as they will see eye to eye on this side of things.

Their sex life should burn fiercely, for a strong physical attraction will exist. Desires and passions are shared and understood, and this may prevent their relationship from deteriorating into some kind of war game. Should Mr. and Ms. Scorpio be of the higher type, they will work at their sex life until they reach five-star rating.

Altogether, a nerve-tearing relationship.

Scorpio Woman with Sagittarius Man

It is difficult to imagine what could possibly bring these two totally opposed personalities together unless it is a physical attraction, in which case it is unlikely to last more than a couple of weeks. Her desire to possess people she loves and manipulate them he will refuse to take seriously, and in any event her attempts to achieve this with him will be completely wasted. It is impossible for any one female to tame this man, especially by force. He loves to chase adventure, of any kind, and will take daily gambles which can reduce this woman to a neurotic, nervous wreck. She will have to be prepared to handle all money matters—as unobtrusively as possible —and she would be unwise to delude herself into thinking that he can ever be a reasonable and serious man. The intensity of Ms. Scorpio's emotions could depress and irritate him as his own feelings are more lighthearted and adaptable. The Scorpio woman is usually engrossed in her career and she can expect encouragement and enthusiasm from Mr. Sagittarius, but she will disapprove of his own checkered career.

Sexually, once more she will believe that he belongs to her and her alone, and once she has made this clear he will rebel and proceed to bed-hop at the first opportunity. He could end up staying away from her for increasingly long periods of time. The Scorpio woman, who in general enjoys a drink, could well be driven to the bottle by this man.

A turbulent relationship.

Scorpio Woman with Capricorn Man

Her need for security and peace may account for her attraction to Mr. Capricorn, while he may be attracted to what he believes is a strong, uncomplicated woman. After a while the complexity of her personality will begin to sink in and he could find the intensity of her emotions quite staggering. The Scorpio woman may have thought that she would be the most important thing in his life, and her jealousy will soon be aroused when he appears to devote most of his waking hours to his career and ambitions. Although initially sympathetic to this, she will eventually become overdemanding in an attempt to attract his attention. Agreement will be reached over their mutual need for a stable background, she enjoys making life comfortable for him and he will appreciate the effort she makes. Financial security is a driving force in both personalities, so conflict in this direction is unlikely.

She may discover not only the man but also his career occupying their bed. Her sex drive is greater than his, and she will need to control it if she is not to make them both unhappy. This man's thoughts are never far away from work, and when living with him this must be accepted.

A relationship which needs hard work but which could succeed.

Scorpio Woman with Aquarius Man

Mr. Aquarius has a strong dislike of drama or trauma in any guise, and the intense emotional scenes that are so much a part of Ms. Scorpio's life could leave him completely cold. He will not argue with her but will begin to wonder whether she is not unbalanced. His continual involvement in the outside world could also threaten their relationship for she prefers him to be exclusively hers and will not share him willingly. The tension may be eased at times when she realizes that he regards her not simply as his lover but also as his friend. If success is to be achieved this could be the basis on which to build a stronger relationship. Just living from day to day is going to be hard work—unless this can be accepted, she is going to start looking around for someone else. Her tendency towards strong likes and dislikes needs to be controlled for the Aquarian man can be equally positive in his opinions, and if he makes her unhappy she may indulge in excess emotion or drink, losing the respect of a man who believes in moderation.

The Scorpio's materialistic view of life could meet with his scorn, he values people and not objects, and cannot understand her constant worrying over financial matters. Jealousy is deeply ingrained in most Scorpios, and his total lack of this emotion could make her feel that his love for her is inadequate.

Again, her sex drive is far more demanding than his so more problems are bound to crop up. There could be many occasions when she will feel neglected, not to say frustrated, and she will feel justified in accusing him of not loving her enough. He will find this exhausting and irritating.

A union best avoided.

Scorpio Woman with Pisces Man

The combination of these two signs could make for a dramatic but in general successful relationship, for neither party is ruled by common sense, rather their actions in life are motivated by intense emotions. The Scorpio gift for delving and probing into everyone with whom he or she comes into contact can make it easier for her than most to understand the more secretive side of Mr. Pisces. She must try to accept that he is not so positive as she is, and where she may be tempted to apply pressure, persuasion could achieve better results. The Piscean character can make him evasive and indecisive which on occasions could lead to her accusing him of being weak. She may resent the popularity he enjoys socially for she finds it difficult to be as effortlessly charming as he is. She will also need to exercise control over her critical eye as this man can sink into deep depression when his faults are laid open for all to see. She must also be prepared to take control of the financial side of their life as Mr. Pisces' inclination to dream makes it difficult for him to look at life practically. She could be more successful in her career than he for the Piscean man is rarely consumed with ambition; she may resent this as she believes the man should assume the role of provider. It may be possible for them to overcome these differences as the emotional side of life should be so compatible as to make it impossible for them to drift apart for any length of time.

Emotions are dramatized in the bedroom as both soon realize that this can stimulate their sexual appetites and heighten pleasure. The Scorpio jealousy will be lovingly calmed by this understanding man. This relationship generally works out better with a reversed combination of signs, but success can be achieved with hard work.

An emotionally charged relationship.

Scorpio Woman with Aries Man

This threatens to be a Martian type of relationship with the emphasis on conflict, collision and war. Both partners are born fighters, but where in most cases they would take on the whole world in an effort to defend their relationship, in this instance they are likely to turn on one another. Where generally the Arietian male will at least listen to another person's point of view, Ms. Scorpio's own stubborn refusal to accept that she might be wrong will make him just as bloodyminded as she is. Attitudes to work inevitably clash, for where she believes that a man should stay in the same job for life working his way up from teaboy to managing director, he will change direction whenever a new or more exciting challenge presents itself. His belief in living in the present will make him shortsighted to their future financial security, and when she applies pressure on him over this she will be faced with fiery outbursts of rage. The Arietian male prefers to dispense with emotion wherever possible for he believes it restricts the individual, and her emotionally charged ravings he will find neurotic and unnecessary.

There are days when their sex life can work out wonderfully and others when they will lie brooding on their respective sides of the bed. If they have had a row, Ms. Scorpio will find it very hard to forgive and forget, and although initially he will try to coax her out of this unrelenting mood the impatient Arietian cannot be expected to put up with this for very long. A woman such as this, with fixed ideas and a strong need for security, cannot in general find fulfillment in partnership with an Arietian male.

An unwise relationship. These two characters will find it difficult to be friends let alone lovers.

Scorpio Woman with Taurus Man

Both these characters can be immovably stubborn, set in their opinions and beliefs. This can make for many problems, and ideally each should find a more flexible lover. Their stubbornness can reflect onto all aspects of their relationship, even minor issues such as which film to go and see can cause war to be declared, and the more serious issues in life will be made intolerable. Financial problems are unlikely to arise, however, as they both have a commonsense approach to money. And their jealousy could also bring them closer together, as each will understand the feelings of insecurity which give rise to possessiveness. The need for a stable background and domestic environment is an inescapable part of both personalities and will play a large part in their life together. These common attitudes are the only hope for them, but the fixed mind continually threatens to make it difficult for them to work on their relationship in a light-hearted and unprejudiced way. Yet one more cause of tension is the strong emotional nature of the Scorpio in confrontation with the realistic, rational side of the Taurean.

She may at times complain about his lack of imagination in bed, but if she remembers to take the lead more often he may come to appreciate what is missing from his own approach. Their sex life will still be erratic, however, for though both have active sexual appetites the occasions when desires coincide could be few.

This is a good business partnership but it is unwise to attempt a personal relationship.

Scorpio Woman with Gemini Man

If Mr. Gemini meets Ms. Scorpio while in a depressed state of mind he will be attracted to her strength, perception and intensity, but when he is back on his feet and ready to once more bounce back into life he may find that she is reluctant to let him go. Once he has started a relationship with her she will expect to take complete possession, and when he airs his objections to this he will be greeted with an unpleasant emotional scene. The Scorpio's need for financial security and a calm existence is threatened by such a man. His irresponsibility, crazy ideas and general restlessness can all be relied upon to provide a deep rift in their relationship. Her determination and hatred of being wrong will probably lead her to make attempts at changing him, and although he may try to give the impression that he is willing to become more the type of man she believes he should be this is only superficial and he will go his own way at the first opportunity. With time he could come to regard her as neurotic, bigoted and a chain around his neck. Once he starts trying to break free there will be little she can do to restrain him.

The mental stimulation Mr. Gemini needs to trigger his sexual appetite will go unrecognized by Ms. Scorpio, his restlessness will merely serve to confuse and worry her. Eventually, she will realize that she has been unwise in this choice of lover, and unless she is specifically looking for a difficult, lonely life she will start looking elsewhere.

This combination of characters would be best avoided.

Scorpio Woman with Cancer Man

Mr. Cancer could be exactly the man Ms. Scorpio is looking for; he too is strongly influenced by his emotions, and his sensitivity allows him to appreciate even the slightest variation of her moods. His ability to give is desperately needed by the strong, fixed Scorpio woman. She will always feel emotionally secure in the devotion he constantly showers on her, and this can do much to contribute to the calming of her jealous and suspicious nature. For most of the time he will be happy to let her have her own way, and because of this her stubborn streak can on occasions become diluted, she will gradually become more resilient and may even try to see his point of view.

In a quieter way Mr. Cancer is just as concerned as she is about financial problems, and he plans accordingly; debt-collectors and bailiffs are unlikely to intrude upon their life. To him the home is all-important and he will be happy to sit and watch her do her "little woman" thing around the home. These moments can serve to bring them even closer together. Social life is unlikely to be a problem as interests will always be shared, although they are both content to spend a quiet evening at home together.

Their sex life is unlikely to be dull, for their physical

relationship will rest on emotions which are forever changing and developing together. Mutual desires, passions and needs should find satisfaction in this relationship, without the traumas and suspicions that plague them with another partner.

A splendid union.

Scorpio Woman with Leo Man

At first Mr. Leo will give all of his warmth and generosity to his Scorpio woman, but when he realizes she can be just as strong as he his role as the leader in the partnership may seem threatened and he could become arrogant and overbearing. Both have a natural urge to dominate and their relationship could deteriorate into a battlefield. Her "always right" attitude will infuriate him for, although he may not realize this, it is very similar to his own. The Leo man usually prefers his woman to remain in the background and supply him with all the encouragement and admiration he desperately needs, but a Scorpio cannot be overlooked or kept down and she will rise in rebellion against him. The lazy side to his character is incomprehensible to her and she may attempt to bully him out of these moods, but the Leo cannot be moved until he is ready and she will only meet with frustration in these efforts.

His extravagance will threaten her need for security and many an argument could rage over money. If any sort of harmony is to be achieved then one of them will have to surrender his or her bid for the role of leader.

As this is unlikely to occur, lengthy relationships with this combination of characters are uncommon.

Sex may contribute towards cementing their union for they can both be intense and passionate and will at least agree on the importance of a good and active sex life. Without compatibility in bed, this relationship can have little to offer either party as mentally they are poles apart.

Scorpio Woman with Virgo Man

Although Ms. Scorpio enjoys the power she derives from her ability to analyze and understand people almost at a glance, her superiority in this field is threatened by the critical Virgo eye which classifies and dissects all that it observes. This will of course include her, and as a Scorpio can never bear to think that she is imperfect this is likely to be the biggest stumbling-block to harmony. She is proud of her good health and will not appreciate his continual fussing whenever she looks off-color, for she will not realize that it makes him feel important to care and tend for those he loves. Emotionally, life could be difficult for while to her each day is a new emotional experience his days are spent attempting to improve himself intellectually, therefore her dramatic outbursts are greeted by his cool reasoning which refuses to become unruffled—infuriating for her.

The Virgo's industrious and conscientious work-pattern will meet with approval from this woman, however, and his practical, realistic attitude to money will at least give her peace of mind where finances are con-

cerned. This is probably the only side of life on which
they will agree, therefore it should be developed and
made the most of.

Their sexual appetites differ, which does not help.
Often, he can seem cold and unable to satisfy the emotion that is welling up inside of her. This could lead to
her bottling-up her feeling and eventually turning to
another man as a safety-valve, for it is either this or a
tendency to be self-destructive.

In general, this union has far too much against it for
it to succeed.

Scorpio Woman with Libra Man

A woman as complex as Ms. Scorpio, one who takes a
considerable amount of time to understand, could appeal to the Libran love of challenge. He will enjoy
learning something new about her every day and will
try his best to put this knowledge to use within their
relationship. Their troubles could stem from their opposing attitudes to home life; he cannot become a domestic body and will resent any attempt by her to try to
change him in this respect. Because of this, he could
come to realize how fixed and determined she can be,
and her emotional outbursts will seem ugly to a man
such as he who needs harmony and beauty around him.
He will not indulge in arguments or fights but will simply go out and not return until he feels she will be in a
more reasonable frame of mind, and with every repeated incident of this sort they will grow further and

further apart, until inevitably the time will come when he stays out all night long. The Libran man will not spend his time worrying about money for this is unpleasant and he hates unpleasantness. His unrealistic attitude here will aggravate the Scorpio's fear of financial insecurity.

Mental stimulation, glamour, novelty and romance all play their part in his sex life, and all this is likely to confuse her. But her stubborn ways make it impossible for her to give in this direction, and when she finds out that he has been driven to seek satisfaction in another woman's bed the Scorpian jealousy will flare up and tear their relationship to shreds.

An unlikely and incompatible relationship.

ARE YOU A TYPICAL SCORPIO MAN?

Answer the questions below honestly, using Yes, No and Sometimes, then turn to page 305 for the answer.

1. Are you jealous?

2. Have you fixed opinions?

3. Do you enjoy your drink?

4. Are you stubborn?

5. Do you demand loyalty from your women?

6. Are you offended when rebuffed sexually?

7. Do you bear grudges?

8. Do you use sex as a form of self-expression?

9. Are you capable of using a woman physically if it suits you?

10. Do you always understand your mate's sexual needs?

11. Are you sarcastic?

12. Do homosexuals disgust you?

13. Would you take revenge on an old enemy if the chance presented itself?

14. Can you be violent when deeply stirred?

15. Are you suspicious of strangers without sufficient reason?

16. Do you think a woman's place is in the home?

17. Can you be destructive?

18. Are you proud of your good health?

19. Does laziness irritate you?

20. Is it hard for you to fall in love?

Total up your score, allowing three for a Yes, two for a Sometimes and one for a No, then turn to page 305.

ARE YOU A TYPICAL SCORPIO WOMAN?

Answer the questions below honestly, using Yes, No and Sometimes, then turn to page 306 for the answer.

1. Is it hard for you to fall in love?

2. Does your intuition reveal the faults of others?

3. Are you of a jealous disposition?

4. When desperate for affection will you sleep with almost anyone?

5. Are weak men attracted to you?

6. Do you need a loyal man?

7. Is it hard for you to express your desires in bed?

8. Is it hard for you to forgive and forget?

9. Can you be aggressive in bed?

10. Are you hypersensitive?

11. Is it hard for others to get to know the real you?

12. Do you think teenage brides are making a mistake?

13. Do you become highly nervous when run-down?

14. Do you enjoy a drink?

15. Are you good with finances?

16. Are you reluctant to change your job?

17. Are you a good judge of character?

18. Do you think a regular sex life is very important?

19. Is it hard for you to make new friends?

20. Does your imagination do most of the work for
     you in bed?

*Total up your score, allowing three for a Yes, two for a
Sometimes and one for a No, then turn to page 306.*

SAGITTARIUS

THE ARCHER

The Sign of the Sage
or Counsellor

November 23rd to December 21st

THE THIRD FIRE SIGN: *Candid, restless, impatient, curious, impulsive, nature- and sport-lover*

RULER: *Jupiter*   **GEMS:** *Carbuncle, turquoise*

COLOR: *Light blue*   **METAL:** *Tin*

Characteristics of the Higher Male

This sign endows great mental ability on its subjects, enabling them to bring their reason to bear upon everything they behold. Mr. Sagittarius is stimulated when in the process of exploring and digging down to the bottom of things, condensing them to the simplest terms. His mental vigor never tires, his curiosity is rarely satisfied. This man is a formidable antagonist, foolish objections and suggestions are met with little mercy from him, for he has an intuition that allows him to seek out his adversary's weakest point, and once this has been accomplished he knows exactly what actions are called for. This tendency can lead him successfully into the legal profession, literature and journalism. Hobbies normally take the Sagittarian male outside, golf, fishing and football all appeal, for he revels in the open-air and stale rooms or stuffy atmospheres are quite uncongenial to him.

This individual is the truth-seeker, and his probing mind may often offend some of his friends, for the more they hide the more persistent he becomes. In childhood he is most difficult to handle, restraint produces in him resentment and rebellion, as his love of freedom is well-developed and as a rule will stay with him throughout life.

A man who is forever trying to learn comes constantly in touch with his fellow man and a lonely Sagittarian is rare indeed. His characteristic frankness and outspoken manner are carried through to his friendships and love attachments, but in the latter this tendency is likely to cause trouble rather than dispel it, for above all he is an honest man, even where it can hurt deeply. Mr. Sagittarius admits to having loved before and will normally go on to add that no doubt he will love again; the female concerned should either accept probable disloyalty or forget him. This man should ideally choose a partner on the same mental plane as himself without ignoring the question of temperament and character; instead, he is usually attracted to glamor alone, although he will soon come to realize that any female who is to put up with him for life will need far more than a pretty face. Once this character has been disappointed or hurt in love, he can react by forming relationships with females who cannot threaten his freedom and married women may become a hard to break habit with him.

No female can take this man and shut him away for herself, but if she insists, while appearing to succumb to her wishes, he will in truth either look around for a more open-minded companion or hurl sarcasm at her until all that is left of their union is a shaky physical relationship, soon to die. He needs someone in sympathy with his desire to communicate and flirt, someone who is as wide awake as he is himself.

Many men born under this sign shun marriage completely, for the love of being their own master is powerful, but once mated suitably he can be happy and children will adore a father who is in possession of so much spirit and love of adventure.

His career may bring him much success for this is a lucky man and one who can bring success out of failure time and time again. This, together with his charm and gift for clever conversation, can take him far.

Characteristics of the Higher Female

The same dangers that threaten the male confront the female of this sign. Her frank, open ways are often misconstrued, for the friendship she offers is frequently taken for love, and although her need of freedom and honesty can initially attract the male sex, this attraction will only last until they realize she cannot be changed. As a rule, when facing a crisis brought about in this way she can adapt and has a happy knack of turning the situation into a joke, one which the hurt suitor can appreciate and which soothes his damaged pride. Unfortunately, should this situation recur often, Ms. Sagittarius may eventually find difficulty in allowing her true self to show and, like her male counterpart, could resort to relationships which cannot tie her. She needs a man who will not take offense every time she smiles or dances with another, a special kind of man who can love enough to allow her to be herself and not try to possess her body and soul.

When the man and time are right she is capable of becoming a devoted mother, one who will behave more as a big sister to the children, and because of this a close bond could exist between them all.

Characteristics of the Lower Type

In this individual the love of freedom will become distorted, and he will be boorish or rude to any female whom he regards as his equal and therefore a threat to his liberty. Such a man behaves in an over-familiar and liberty-taking manner with those he considers unable to trap him.

Because of his absorption in the present, loyalty and faithful companionship are alien to him. One result of this is a lack of consideration for others; reputation means nothing to him, neither his own nor his fellow creatures', and these tendencies may lead to a complete lack of moral behavior and to the suffering of many who cross his path. The danger, however, is sometimes minimized due to this subject's transparency—only those who wish to be deceived are his victims, for the absence of complex emotion and total lack of jealousy can be relied upon to give him away. Add to this the inability to lie successfully and you have a pretty obvious male. This is the sign of the truth-seeker and even this lower type cannot deceive convincingly.

Physical Characteristics

The Sagittarian is recognized by his well-shaped head and breadth of forehead, his frank and open manner, quick movements and vigorous gestures. Although expressive, a lack of grace is evident bordering on clumsiness. The eyes are bright, twinkling with fun, and observant, taking in all at a glance.

Two types are characteristic to this sign, one tall and athletic, commanding in stature, the second short, broad shouldered and thick-set, growing fat in old age. The true subject is restless and unable to keep still. There is a disregard of convention, much self-confidence and an ability to be conspicuous.

Their health is good, with the exception of over-activity reacting on nerves. A typical feature is an unusually long thigh bone.

SAGITTARIUS MALE

	Sex	Love	Marriage	Business	Friends (opposite sex)	Friends (same sex)
ARIES		•	•	•		•
TAURUS					•	
GEMINI	•				•	•
CANCER						
LEO		•	•	•	•	•
VIRGO						
LIBRA	•					
SCORPIO						
SAGITTARIUS	•				•	•
CAPRICORN						
AQUARIUS					•	
PISCES	•					

SAGITTARIUS FEMALE

	Sex	Love	Marriage	Business	Friends (opposite sex)	Friends (same sex)
ARIES		•	•	•	•	•
TAURUS	•			•	•	•
GEMINI	•					
CANCER						
LEO		•	•	•		•
VIRGO						
LIBRA	•					
SCORPIO						
SAGITTARIUS	•				•	•
CAPRICORN						
AQUARIUS				•		
PISCES	•					

SAGITTARIUS MAN tends to be either very tall or very short, with a slim body and long thighs; a broad forehead, often with a receding hairline; bright eyes, a snub nose and a wide, frank mouth.

SAGITTARIUS WOMAN tends to have a long-waisted body with good legs and figure; light-colored hair; an open, honest face with a snub nose, thin eyebrows and a kind mouth.

THE SAGITTARIUS PARTNERSHIPS

Sagittarius Woman with Sagittarius Man

These two could be brought together by their common tendency to treat relationships in a lighthearted manner. They each respect the other's driving need for personal freedom, and it is possible that for the first time in their lives they will feel totally free to go their own way while at the same time retaining a good relationship with one particular member of the opposite sex. Their social life must be hectic for Sagittarius attracts other people, and while this will suit both of them they may suddenly come to realize that their moments alone together are few. A love of the outdoors may mean that they can be together while participating in some sporting activity. A characteristic strong in both is an insistence on the truth, and while this may seem ideal it can in fact lead to problems, for after a while details of the other's affairs can begin to niggle and hurt. Also, the blatantly candid way that faults are discussed could deepen the wound or could add a streak of sensitivity normally alien to this sign.

The biggest danger, however, to this relationship is that the thing which brought them together could drive them apart; they may become so involved in their own separate lives that they could almost forget the existence of the other, and then it would not take much to break them up. Two irresponsible people with a tendency to gamble with life can lead to constant financial difficulty, and although threatening letters and legal writs fail to distress either partner unduly there must come a point when these problems overwhelm them.

Sexually, this is a versatile combination, both minds are open to experiment and so anything is possible— anyone for an orgy? Providing they are able to make one another feel important and do not ruin the other's ego through playing it too cool, this could be a fitting relationship for them both.

Sagittarius Woman with Capricorn Man

While going through one of her many periods of financial difficulty Ms. Sagittarius will be impressed by the practical outlook on life displayed by Mr. Capricorn. He may find that in her company her carefree personality can take his mind off the many worries and pressures he invariably suffers from. But after a while, these are the very things which could cause trouble. He may come home one evening and find that she has spent the money allocated for food on a sexy nightdress that took her fancy, and when he fails to admire it and can only think instead of his empty stomach she will call him a drag and a bore. The Capricorn difficulty in expressing deep emotion may frustrate her for her outgoing and honest nature demands expression of all experience. The Sagittarian capacity for enjoyment and general belief that life's a gas cannot fail to collide with his serious, reserved and pessimistic outlook. When going through one of his black depressions he can expect little sympathy from this woman for she can see nothing to get depressed about and refuses to look on the gloomy side of anything.

More problems can be expected in the physical side of their life; she may welcome him home in some sexually inviting outfit, perfumed from head to toe and all set to seduce him, and he will calmly walk in, open his briefcase and proceed to work on some problem connected with work without giving her a second glance. Although on occasions they can get together sexually, on its own this is insufficient to bridge the gaps in their relationship, and the constant tension must eventually affect their sex life in a detrimental way.

A frustrating partnership.

Sagittarius Woman with Aquarius Man

Ms. Sagittarius' free and independent outlook on life can attract the Aquarian man as this seems to coincide with his own attitude. He loathes the weaker and more clinging type of woman, she cramps his style. His constant involvement in the outside world is fine with her for she too believes in living life to the full, and although the company of others is appreciated by both many of their evenings may be separately enjoyed for he tries to reform and help his fellow men where she simply enjoys their company and tries to learn from them. There are occasions, however, when she may need him, and when he is not there she could feel neglected and unloved. This could be the result of his inability to be demonstrative, and while feeling the need for a warmer personality she may meet a different character who could be the beginning of a series of affairs. Neither partner finds it easy to plan for the financial future, but possibly the Aquarian personality is better equipped to cope and therefore it is he who should make an effort in this direction.

She is completely free from any sexual inhibitions and hang-ups, and is an altogether warmer person than he is. His complete trust in her and total lack of jealousy may lead her to believe that he does not care for her deeply, and eventually another man will find it easy to tempt her away from him.

An emotionally uncomfortable relationship.

Sagittarius Woman with Pisces Man

Although each may be attracted to the charm displayed by the other, underneath this their personalities are very different. Her frank, candid and open approach to living is hard for this man to understand for he is more complex and can be more easily influenced by prevailing circumstances or by those around him. She will be hurt when he withdraws into his own secretive world, making it obvious that she is not included in his thoughts, and when she attempts to draw him out, however persuasively, he will refuse to respond until it suits him. The direct way that she can follow a train of thought is also alien to the Piscean who finds it difficult to sustain or follow anything through to its conclusion. Decisions will rest with her; normally she would avoid them, but his hopeless indecisiveness will make it obvious that this is the only alternative. Her optimistic mind and his pessimism can also add to the tension as each will find the other's attitude incomprehensible. These incompatibilities may be further aggravated by financial difficulties as neither is really equipped to cope with these. He tends to shut his mind off from unpleasant realities and her optimistic faith refuses to accept the fact that things are really bad.

Sex may bring them closer together because it is equally important to both. She is very active sexually and will willingly go along with his love of fantasy. But a purely physical relationship cannot survive for long on its own, and they will start looking for someone who can make them happy outside as well as inside bed.

A confusing relationship which is unlikely to bring contentment to either party.

Sagittarius Woman with Aries Man

Although she may be instantly attracted to Mr. Aries, Ms. Sagittarius will sense his desire to possess and dominate her. If she is wise, she will cool her emotions while trying to decide whether or not she can accept this, but his strength and warmth of personality will no doubt prove irresistible to her. She is likely to decide that she can for once allow herself to be tied to another. When he comes to her with new ideas on how to improve their lot she will offer her enthusiasm no matter how many times his ideas amount to nothing, and he could come to rely on her optimism to boost his sagging ego when things do not go according to plan. The Arietian finds it difficult to plan for the financial future sensibly, but as Ms. Sagittarius is so hopelessly impractical he will need to take the responsibility on to his own shoulders, or financial difficulty could undermine their otherwise satisfactory relationship.

Their sex life should work out fine, providing they are able to find the time to go to bed, as so much outside activity could threaten the importance of sex in their union. Normally a very active woman in this direction, Ms. Sagittarius could in this relationship channel her appetites elsewhere and hardly notice that she is doing so, their life will be so full.

A happy relationship.

Sagittarius Woman with Taurus Man

Their opposing attitudes to life could superficially attract, as at the beginning of a relationship the stronger differences may not be evident. He is attracted to this humorous, lighthearted and bubbly woman, half-wishing he too could be as carefree. She on the other hand could find his practical realism and serious outlook a refreshing change from the usual type of man with whom she gets involved. Later, however, these mutually attracting traits will provide the basis for conflict. Overnight, he will realize that he can never possess her wholly for love of freedom is too deeply ingrained in her, and his down-to-earth manner, never varying from day to day, she will eventually come to look on as sheer boredom. His jealousy could be the beginning of the end for them and in open defiance of his possessiveness she will flirt with any man near at hand. Financially, she could aggravate his carefulness into becoming meanness, as he constantly worries about financial security and she cannot see the need for such concern.

Assuming that she loves him sufficiently not to launch herself into a string of affairs, she may at least like to think and speak about others while making love. Mr. Taurus, with his lack of imagination, will tend to take this literally, or will at least place too much importance on it, and life could become impossible for them.

A frustrating and nerve-racking partnership.

Sagittarius Woman with Gemini Man

In this relationship the emphasis must be on fun and novelty and excitement, both having over-active, intelligent and communicative minds which needs regular exercise. Both attract plenty of friends and they can expect to spend little time alone in their home. The separate lives they are free to lead and the unrestricting personalities of each can keep them contented and happy with one another for a while.

Life could be made uncomfortable by the constant knock of creditors on their front door, and although this may be treated as a huge joke at first, sooner or later they will realize that something must be done—the problem being, who is going to do it. It may fall to her to attempt to sort out the mess they have both got into for he is unlikely to take the situation seriously or even want to discuss it.

Career-wise, it is difficult to imagine either of them in a steady job for long, it is more likely that she will provide for six months or so until the Geminian suddenly decides to take over this role for a short time, and so on.

Their sex life may take on an unreal appearance for both need mental stimulation and novelty, and they may resort to extreme fantasy in an effort to create this and be happy. Infidelity is not regarded as a deadly sin and it will be a rare occasion when a third party is not intervening in their relationship.

A good relationship for a short time, but as a rule each would be wiser to choose a steadier partner for anything more than an affair.

Sagittarius Woman with Cancer Man

Mr. Cancer will be attracted to the Sagittarian's charming and sociable manner, and while listening to her ideas on freedom and individuality he will delude himself into believing that this is just an image she tries to project and that underneath is a feminine woman looking for the right man. His sensitivity and devotion may hold her interest for a while, she probably thinks that this gentle man will be easy to manage.

It will not be long, however, before they both realize the mistakes they have made. This woman cannot revolve her life around him and their home, for her domestic impulses are practically non-existent. When she is suddenly confronted by the tenacious side of Mr. Cancer she will wonder what happened to the sensitive and pliable person she met. His tendency to stay at home watching the television or reading can be relied upon to drive her insane, staying at home to her is only necessary when ill or when there is absolutely nothing better to do—which is rare, for her outside interests constantly tempt her away. His financial shrewdness will be misconstrued as penny-pinching, and she could go out of her way to be extravagant.

They are not especially well-suited sexually, either, for he is too intense and romantic for her, but a lot depends on how deeply her love goes. If he is devoted, which he could well be, she may come to understand that she can twist him round her little finger where sex is concerned, but once she tires of this game she will reach out for a more challenging prospect, leaving a disillusioned and shattered man behind her.

Normally, her feelings do not go deep enough to overcome the obstacles of this union.

Sagittarius Woman with Leo Man

Mr. Leo may have watched Ms. Sagittarius for some time before making his move, in which case he will have observed her effect on the opposite sex and the line of admirers she invariably seems to have in tow. The Leo tendency to always want the best in life may lead him to believe that a woman in such demand must belong in this category, and when he finally makes his move she will not have time to gather her thoughts or protest at all. Although initially taken aback by such an over-powering man, she will soon come to realize that it is quite reassuring and flattering to have so much atten-tion, warmth and generosity overwhelming her. Whereas with a different character this would create instant rebellion in her, the masculinity of Mr. Leo is hard to resist. His pride may be the reason for their first argument, for if he sees her admiring another man he will become extremely indignant and may even termi-nate their relationship, for he cannot tolerate competi-tion. If this should happen she will be left with a cold and empty void in her life and could well make at-tempts to regain his love despite the sacrifices involved. If she can manage to handle his ego and pride carefully, he may recognize her need for personal freedom provid-ing this does not involve other men. The Leo man will love to show her off to his friends and will enjoy buying her things, this in turn must make her feel well-loved.

Basically a very animalistic woman in bed, it is more than likely that she will learn to love emotionally from this man. Their sexual appetites being very well devel-oped, they will spend a lot of time happily in bed. He will not tolerate any infidelity on her part, of course, but with him she could well be content.

An excellent partnership.

Sagittarius Woman with Virgo Man

The minds of these two people work at very different speeds and go off in very different directions. His actions are generally guided by cool intellect and reason, and the material, financial side of life is invariably top of his list of priorities, while Ms. Sagittarius will act from feeling or impulse. These differences may at first attract as each could be curious to learn about somebody so totally unlike themselves, but no matter how long they are together it is doubtful if they will ever really come to understand one another. Their opposing financial outlooks will be hard to reconcile. The constant activity that surrounds this woman will irritate the Virgo man, he may wish to spend an evening working on office papers only to find himself surrounded by half a dozen of her friends she has neglected to mention were coming. It is possible that Ms. Sagittarius may attempt to discuss their problems but this could well result in her becoming more aware of their incompatibility. She may try to achieve some response by abuse, which will only be met by a cold indifference. This could trigger off her first affair outside this relationship.

His sexual appetite is no match for hers, and their sex life will not contribute to a peaceful existence—he is likely to conclude that she is over-demanding and sex-mad. A conclusion guaranteed to drive her into behavior which will only substantiate his beliefs.

Possibly a good friendship, but a close relationship ill-advised.

Sagittarius Woman with Libra Man

The active social life of both characters in this combination may account for their attraction and meeting. The Libran, who hates disharmony, will be attracted to this woman who appears to be so lighthearted and gay for the majority of the time, while she will enjoy his romantic approach and his eloquent gift for making her feel feminine and desirable.

This could prove to be quite an exhausting relationship as both have many interests and friends and each will attempt to introduce the other to them. Some trouble may arise here as their circles are comprised of such different types of people—she is more attracted to the sporting, casual type while he is attracted to the sophisticated, artistic and elegant. There may be some unpleasantness over her unsophisticated appearance, he will try to persuade her to become more polished, but it is possible to reach a compromise on this point without too much friction. Their financial situation threatens to be precarious, the Sagittarian woman cannot be made to face a financial crisis and although normally prone to running away from such things himself Mr. Libra could find that he has, however reluctantly, to assume responsibility in these matters.

Although this is not an ideal relationship, their sexual attraction could be strong and their appetites equal. Mr. Libra will enjoy making her satisfied, tackling this in a good-humored and tolerant way, and his attitude could well be infectious.

An eventful partnership.

Sagittarius Woman with Scorpio Man

Mr. Scorpio's suspicious nature makes it difficult for him to mix socially or enjoy popularity, he is therefore drawn to this woman who mixes so freely and attracts so much good feeling from others. He could feel that by being with her he will improve his social standing, neglecting to make allowances for his jealousy, while his intensity and difficulty in relaxing may be something new to her. She can sense the depth of feeling in him and will believe that in time this may find expression, but the Scorpio man can never tell her of his inner emotions and his strong jealousy is the only outlet for such intensity. Although she may feel flattered and important to begin with, later her desire for freedom will begin to grow and she will search for a way to escape. Many arguments will ensue because of this despite the fact that up till now his feelings of insecurity have been unfounded. A glance at another man or an interest in another man's achievements are enough to light the fuse, and even though he may realize he is only driving her away he will not be able to control himself.

Financially, the Scorpio needs to know where he stands, he plans for the future and pays bills promptly, and any small extravagance on her part is sufficient to instigate an argument.

Although straightforward, their sex life is likely to be

passionate and could help to hold her interest in him a little longer. But they cannot spend all day and all night in bed, and must get up to face their personality problems some time.

A stormy relationship can be predicted, with only a small ray of hope for success.

ARE YOU A TYPICAL SAGITTARIAN MAN?

Answer honestly the questions below, using Yes, No or Sometimes, then turn to page 307 for the answer.

then turn to page 307 for the answer.

1. Is it hard for you to relinquish your personal freedom?

2. Is fidelity difficult for you to achieve?

3. Do you take part in some sport?

4. Do you chase get-rich-quick schemes?

5. Does jealousy in others bore you?

6. Are you lucky?

7. Is it hard for you to budget?

8. Do you think it is perfectly natural to try all sexual experience?

9. Would you drop your girl if she became possessive?

10. Does the thought of staying in the same job for twenty years depress you?

11. Are you free from inhibition?

12. Do you speak rapidly?

13. Are you clumsy?

14. Do you think marriage is old-fashioned?

15. Can you indulge in three or four affairs at the same time without feeling guilty?

16. Do small-minded people annoy you?

17. Does routine bore you?

18. Are children excluded from your plans?

19. Is it hard for you to remember birthdays?

20. Are you attracted to married women?

Total up your score, allowing three for Yes, two for Sometimes and one for No, then turn to page 307.

ARE YOU A TYPICAL SAGITTARIAN WOMAN?

Answer honestly the questions below, using Yes, No or Sometimes, then turn to page 308 for the answer.

1. Do you think you will ever surrender your personal freedom?

2. Does jealousy kill love for you?

3. Do married or attached men attract you?

4. Would you do anything your man wanted in bed?

5. Do you enjoy some outdoor activity?

6. Are you a restless person?

7. Do you need a target in life?

8. Does fidelity come hard to you?

9. Could you sleep with a friend's husband or lover without feeling guilty?

10. Are your physical movements quick?

11. Do crazy and unorthodox ideas appeal to you?

12. Can you get out of one man's bed then leap into another's half an hour later?

13. Do you support Women's Lib?

14. Is your friendly approach to everyone misconstrued by men?

15. Do you have a hectic social life?

16. Do you live in the present for the present?

17. Are you drawn to a man who does not appear to fancy you?

18. Do you hate formal occasions?

19. Are you lucky?

20. Is it hard for you to form a deep and lasting relationship?

Total up your score, allowing three for Yes, two for Sometimes and one for No, then turn to page 308.

CAPRICORN

THE GOAT

The Sign of the Priest, Ambassador, Scientist

December 22nd to January 20th

THE THIRD EARTH SIGN: *Ambitious, diplomatic, persevering, reserved, and afflicted with deep depression*

RULER: *Saturn* GEMS: *White onyx, moonstone*

COLOR: *Green* METAL: *Lead*

Characteristics of the Higher Male

The higher Capricorn is impartial, just and precise. He attempts to achieve accuracy, exactness and consistency in all undertakings and fulfills himself through persistence, industry and endeavor. Such an individual succeeds in bringing economy to a kind of perfection, knowing how to be frugal and thrifty without appearing in the least bit mean.

He will rise through his own effort and personal merit, and although success will normally come late in life for him due to the restricting influences of Saturn, over the years his path will take him steadily upwards.

In the fully evolved type there exists a fine traditional and historic sense, which often finds outlet in a fascination for anything old or in an interest for past event. He could rarely be accused of gambling with his life or indeed with the lives of those for whom he is responsible. Decisions are taken carefully, all considerations being duly noted, and he wisely learns from past mistakes. A fear of debt or dependency on others may give him a somewhat serious outlook that can at times result in deep depression: this is the sign notorious for pessimism and black moods, and in spite of the comfort offered by loved ones the melancholia can only be lifted by the subject himself when he feels ready to cope with life once more.

To some extent external influences will affect his friendships, for one of the vices common to Capricorn is snobbery. Contacts may be judged by their usefulness and he is impressed by rank, wealth or breeding.

Love affairs intrigue this male, though his interest is not merely confined to his own relationships, but also takes in the affairs of others. He is very conscious of the sex difference and can find it difficult to be himself when the opposite sex is around, for he is constantly attempting to project some kind of challenge, provoking many encounters of wit—not always of the most desirable type, as they may be full of innuendo. In youth the Capricorn man is an incorrigible flirt, although in later years this may change and develop into a strong protective instinct, sometimes into patronage.

In general, ambition is the driving force in this subject. Striving to remove unpleasantness from his surroundings, he excels in patching up broken friendships, clearing up misunderstandings and smoothing out tangles in family life. As a rule he makes an excellent parent and a reliable husband, if a somewhat grave and serious one.

Under a façade that tends to be reserved, there lurks a man capable of giving much love—though he does not intend to give it to just anyone, he needs a female who can offer reassurance when life goes against him, who can show him the funnier side of life and who will understand his driving ambition.

This character remembers and observes dates of anniversaries, making much of a special occasion or a social reunion, for he is a generous host and popular in this capacity, besides being a delightful guest. In advancing years he is usually looked up to as an authority on matters of dress or deportment, and is consulted on questions of precedence or social procedure. He can in fact suffer considerably when inadvertently appearing anywhere in unbecoming or unsuitable garments. On the surface Mr. Capricorn may seem to flirt on many social occasions while in truth he is attempting to restore his ever-flagging confidence, and this behavior is rarely sex-motivated. Generally speaking his sexual appetites are of the moderate variety, and it is out of character for him to go to extremes.

Long life can normally be predicted for the Capricorn subject and his most profitable years are often between forty-five and sixty-five.

Characteristics of the Higher Female

As a rule Ms. Capricorn will appear to wear a cool face although, like her brother subject, she has much to give, reaching her warmest peak when married. Ambition plays an important part in her life and her eyes are ever on the search for advancement, which may be her husband's, her children's or her own. So intense is this tendency that there may be sufficient left over for her friends and their families, though her lazy or apathetic fellow man is dealt with in an abrupt, severe manner.

Her friends can recognize the matchmaker in this female and she could give unintentional offense by not minding her own business at times, although interference is not intended, for she is activated either by the desire to see everybody happy or by the wish to help ambition reach fruition. Despondency is her chief enemy and this can drag her down for weeks at a time, the only cure may be a change of environment, cheerful society among friends or an excessive dose of love.

Characteristics of the Lower Type

This character has an uncontrollable urge to manipulate, direct, protect and convert others, and he can soon become notorious as a meddler.

Ambition is blown out of all proportion, his entire

life revolving around it. He may make a mercenary marriage in an effort to further himself, and friendships are based on and valued by their immediate usefulness. This is a social climber who may drive a devoted wife away by sheer neglect.

Physical Characteristics

This type is difficult to classify physically, the most prominent features are a tendency to melancholy, leaden looks, swarthy complexion and sleek, lank, dark hair. Many of these subjects are lively and extremely talkative.

In health matters the black moods can prove to be the most detrimental hazard, for they can directly react on to the physical well-being and the Capricorn should adopt some method that will allow him to step outside his problems, in an attempt to curb this weakness.

CAPRICORN MALE

	Sex	Love	Marriage	Business	Friends (opposite sex)	Friends (same sex)
ARIES						
TAURUS		•	•	•	•	
GEMINI				•		
CANCER				•	•	
LEO				•		
VIRGO	•	•	•	•	•	•
LIBRA						
SCORPIO				•	•	•
SAGITTARIUS						
CAPRICORN	•			•	•	
AQUARIUS						
PISCES	•					•

CAPRICORN FEMALE

	Sex	Love	Marriage	Business	Friends (opposite sex)	Friends (same sex)
ARIES				•		
TAURUS		•	•	•	•	
GEMINI						
CANCER	•					
LEO						
VIRGO	•	•	•	•	•	•
LIBRA						
SCORPIO				•	•	•
SAGITTARIUS						
CAPRICORN	•			•	•	
AQUARIUS						
PISCES						

CAPRICORN MAN tends to have a slim, lively build, short to medium in height; dark, lank hair; a swarthy complexion with round eyes and a slightly worried expression.

CAPRICORN WOMAN tends to have a rather thickset body; lank, rather greasy hair; a long face with heavy features and a leaden, almost melancholic, expression.

THE CAPRICORN PARTNERSHIPS

Capricorn Woman with Capricorn Man

This relationship could well spring from a mutual outlook on life, for both take life seriously and it may be a relief to find another person who approaches every day in a realistic manner. Each believes that hard work is the only possible way to success and although they are ambitious this could lead to problems if their ambitions are channeled into separate careers. Mr. Capricorn gives his work top priority and this can infringe on other aspects of life, for the woman he lives with will need to accept this, placing her own ambitions second to his. This may be very difficult for Ms. Capricorn, as generally she takes a great interest in her own career—and in this case it could be fatal, as too competitive an atmosphere could destroy their relationship.

This is a sign notorious for black and lasting depressions, yet another reason for conflict as each will expect the other to offer consolation and comfort, and should these moods coincide they could easily drift apart. Financial matters are unlikely to create further problems as each is careful and has the ability to save. Capricorn subjects normally need a more light-hearted and sociable partner to prevent them from working too hard or taking life too seriously. This relationship could too easily become stodgy and boring.

The Capricorn's sexual appetite is well-developed but again each needs a more light-hearted partner to arouse interest. Two Capricorns together could well have a non-existent sex life as neither will be capable of turning the other's thoughts from work to bed.

A rather gloomy relationship.

Capricorn Woman with Aquarius Man

Ms. Capricorn may meet this man while going through a bad experience, during which time he is able to offer assistance, for emergencies of all kinds bring out the best in Mr. Aquarius. He may see her depressions initially as some kind of challenge, but when he realizes his optimism and enthusiasm are wasted he could very easily take his sympathy to a more appreciative audience. The Capricorn woman is very much involved in the problems that affect them as a couple and cannot understand the interest he shows in outsiders' troubles, believing that his energy should be used closer to home. He needs and enjoys much social movement, being constantly driven by the desire to exchange ideas. Friends in trouble may descend on them at all hours and will be welcomed with open arms by him while she silently resents the intrusion.

Mr. Aquarius' approach to his career can also irritate for he may go through a number of jobs, always searching for fresh scope and challenge, while she believes he should stay in one place, trying to reach the top and thus giving her security. The Capricorn's desperate need for financial security is incomprehensible to the Aquarian, he cannot be bothered wasting his time worrying about the material side of life.

Sexual clashes are unavoidable, as often when this female is suffering from one of her famous depressions and needs love and reassurance, he will be elsewhere giving this to some worthy cause. Her main problem may be getting him into bed at all. When he is involved in discussing some reform of some kind she may be able to tease him out of this gently and make her desires obvious, but it would be unwise to rely on this as a solution.

Not a satisfactory relationship.

Capricorn Woman with Pisces Man

Mr. Pisces may be drawn to Ms. Capricorn's efficient and well-run life, feeling that his own chaotic situation needs organizing. She could be attracted to his apparent helplessness, but later she will realize that this mood is just one of many, and that in certain frames of mind he can rebel against her attempts to dominate him. It is at this point that his secretive side begins to show, and he may suddenly lapse into a period of silence which can last for days while he is attempting to solve his problems, and no matter how hard she tries she will not be able to overcome the wall he has placed between them.

Depression may also be a cause of friction for the Piscean is also prone to black moods, but where she needs reassurance he prefers to shake his off when he is ready. Just when she has decided that they have made a mistake, he is capable of a complete change in character and can become loving and concerned, giving their relationship a new lease of life. This is a pattern which may be constantly repeated, only ending when she cannot take any more. She must expect to take the lead financially for the Piscean will not wish to be bothered with decisions or the unpleasant side of life.

In general, their sex life should be a close one, although moods could interfere at times, for he is able to switch off problems once in bed where she cannot, and he may eventually decide that she is frigid, without realizing that this is due to mental, not physical, incompatibility. But when both partners are free from depressions their love may be given free expression and this can do much to offset the disadvantages of such a union.

A complex relationship.

Capricorn Woman with Aries Man

Ms. Capricorn may be completely bowled over by Mr. Aries' passionate declarations of love, uttered so quickly after their first meeting, but although initially wary she may interpret his strength of character as security and allow herself to fall in love with him. The first time he becomes enthusiastic about some crazy money-making scheme, however, he will be confronted by her common sense and pessimism. The Arietian male cannot understand and may tease her about her tendency to hide money all over the place, while she could refer to him as "the last of the bigtime spenders." It is unlikely that she will ever learn to adapt to a man forever changing his job and chasing new challenges. She has a deep need for security and only believes that this can be achieved through hard work and routine. It could be that in time he will look for encouragement elsewhere.

Socially, he could be good for her, as his own activity in this field will include her and she may come to realize that there is more to life than work. But the Capricorn woman will automatically respond when the opposite sex is around, and this may stimulate the Arietian jealousy, for he likes to possess his woman body and soul.

Their sex life should be free from serious problems, those that do occur may be connected with her black moods, for he cannot understand them and prefers to believe that if ignored they will go away. His direct approach in bed can be relied upon to offend her at times, especially when in one of her more sensitive moods.

A lengthy relationship is ill-advised.

Capricorn Woman with Taurus Man

The physical attraction could be strong between these two earth subjects, so that the differences between their personalities will be minimized. Although in general not an artistic person, Ms. Capricorn may become so when observing the Taurean man's interest in this direction. Likewise his interest in food can rub off on her as it will be impossible to live with Mr. Taurus without noticing the keen interest he shows in what he eats. The need for a domestic background is shared and each will put much energy into it, drawing strength from each other's interest. The mutual horror of debt will eliminate the possibility of financial difficulty undermining their relationship. They may collect antiques, for both will be interested in the past in some form or another. Their need to get back to nature is also strong and may show in a love of gardening or camping holidays.

Socially, there may be a danger of their being so comfortable at home and so happy in each other's company that they unwittingly cut off the outside world, and this tendency must be fought against before boredom sets in. Ms. Capricorn's ambitions will be encouraged, as long as her career does not overshadow his.

Sexually, this is probably the best relationship for her as he can awake much passion in her where others have failed, and there is a strong possibility that she will learn exactly how to satisfy him.

A happy union.

Capricorn Woman with Gemini Man

It is unlikely that such a combination of characters will be together for longer than a few weeks, attitudes to life being so contradictory, for where the Capricorn prefers to face life squarely and with a realistic eye, the

Geminian prefers to play-act and live his life on impulse. He cannot be made to face up to reality if he does not want to, and this can be for most of the time. She may develop a motherly attitude towards him and learn to protect and build him up when life has treated him badly, for although unaware of it this man is in need of a steady background. He is an emotionally complex man, changing by the hour, and although he can share in her depression it will only be for a short time, and he will expect her to change just as readily. She must expect to take the lead financially for he is generally incapable of budgeting and allowing for bills.

His need for social activity could be good for her and she should allow him to involve her in this way, but her jealousy could be aroused when she realizes that he must flirt with any female between the ages of fifteen and fifty. In most cases this is harmless, just part of the charm. The big danger exists if he comes to regard her serious approach to life as a bore.

Their sex life will bring further trouble, for both are complex, moody, and tend to consider that the other should adapt. Although the Geminian *is* normally an adaptable person, in this case he could become bloodyminded. Only if some kind of compromise can be reached does this union stand a chance of success, but this is unlikely to happen.

A shaky match.

Capricorn Woman with Cancer Man

The Capricorn common sense and energy could well attract the Cancerian sensitivity and intuition. He could be attracted to her while on the rebound from a more impractical type of woman. When her ambitious streak comes to the fore, however, it may worry him as he does not work his best under pressure and finds it unfeminine. On these occasions he may become self-protective, making it impossible for her to communicate with him. His dreamy and romantic frames of mind she may regard as unrealistic and she could unintentionally hurt him by saying so. The Cancer man usually expects his woman to give him strength in the background and will object to her spending so much time on her career, believing this to be a slur on his masculinity and an insult to his role of provider.

Few financial problems should arise as both are shrewd and calculating and capable of saving. No matter how little money they have, a birthday or special occasion will never go unnoticed. This sentimentality is shared and may provide a basis on which to build a closer relationship.

She may need to cultivate her romantic instincts to keep him happy in bed, and he will have to try to accept her reluctance for sex when she is suffering from one of her depressions. He may understand this when not wallowing in self-pity himself, but he is capable of being most obstinate and this could put her off even more.

They will have to strike a balance in their sex life if things are to work out well for them.

A brittle relationship.

Capricorn Woman with Leo Man

Mr. Leo's kindness and generosity, plus his ability to give to those he loves, may be the reason for Ms. Capricorn being attracted to him. He will find it difficult to believe that anybody could be as pessimistic and as serious as she is and may decide that he must take her over and revive her faith in humanity. This, of course, is destined to fail as her realistic appraisal of life is a strong part of her personality and one it is impossible to change.

She may also delude herself by thinking that she can influence him but it would take a very different type of woman to do this. She will disapprove of practically everything he does; his optimism, his ostentation and mad extravagance will all irritate and strengthen her opposite tendencies. Obviously, two people cannot be together overlong without one of them learning to give, but the rebellion between these two could make this impossible. While their illusions remain intact they will survive, but once these are shattered the end cannot be far away. She will probably channel much of her frustration and energy into her career, but here again this must not seem to be more important to her than his.

Mr. Leo likes an active sex life and is very generous with his affections. At times, she will be tempted to make excuses, but this should be avoided as once she has damaged his ego Mr. Leo will be off. It could be a challenging relationship for both as there will be many dramatic scenes in the bedroom; this can either make or break the union.

Capricorn Woman with Virgo Man

Love could spring up pretty quickly between these two characters for they will have an immediate respect for the other's outlook on life. Affection can be hard for them to express with another person, but together their inhibitions should quickly fade away. Virgo man is often accused of cold behavior, and while this may still apply at times for the most part he will be at his warmest with her. He loves to be of assistance and where he can he will offer his enthusiasm and help, especially with her career, in which he will take a great interest. Complete agreement should be achieved over finances, both are interested in money and in saving for the future. Their social life is unlikely to be sophisticated, they share an interest in the outdoors and some healthy activity or sport will usually take preference over a dinner party. The home is also of great importance to both and each will contribute to its comfort and beauty. They will understand each other's need to escape from their environment at times, and separate weekends may occasionally be enjoyed, although these are unlikely to include a third party for Ms. Capricorn and Mr. Virgo are two naturally faithful people.

This relationship is more likely to rest on companionship and mutual interests than on deep passion.

Their sexual appetites are about equal but are never allowed to dominate their life. Suffice to say that this is a happy combination of personalities; although their sex life will be straightforward, this will be ideal for both.

An uncomplicated relationship.

Capricorn Woman with Libra Man

Although Ms. Capricorn will be well aware of Mr. Libra's charm and attraction for the opposite sex, it will still be possible for her to be swept off her feet by him, just as all the others have been. Once they become involved, he could be horrified at her lack of interest in social life; she must either adapt to his constant wish to entertain or be entertained, or expect him to find a more outgoing partner. She may benefit from the wider look at life he can bring to her, and he may become more responsible as time passes, but where he loves to play at love right into advanced age she prefers to take her emotions more seriously. Further clashes will arise over his blind eye concerning her domestic talents, for a ladder in her stocking could provoke more reaction from him than a well-cooked meal.

When their relationship begins to founder, she will be infuriated by the attention he gives to fighting outsiders' battles while appearing indifferent to their own problems. In fact, he will not be indifferent, it is just that his hatred of disharmony in personal relations leads him to ignore an unpleasant atmosphere. Ms. Capricorn's ability with money will be needed to keep them solvent as Mr. Libra prefers to spend without giving a thought to future commitments.

Sexually, his need for mental stimuli and his search for novelty could leave her cold and confused. If she is the only woman in his life at the time he may still enjoy talking of others while making love; this she cannot understand or tolerate, and he will eventually begin to explore more adaptable and interesting terrain.

An unwise union.

Capricorn Woman with Scorpio Man

With the combination of Capricorn and Scorpio, a peaceful co-existence will automatically remain elusive. He has intense likes and dislikes, and believes that he is either loved or hated, and will try to impose his views on her. But her broader and more far-seeing mind will be totally repelled by such beliefs. When he complains of some injustice, real or imaginary, she will take a much more detached view of the situation and may try to point out his mistakes—fatal, for no Scorpio can be made to realize that he was possibly wrong. When this attitude of hers causes him great unhappiness, as it must do, this could provoke in her a patronizing response which will greatly offend his pride. His jealousy and possessiveness will make it impossible for her to have any life of her own, her interest in her career will have to be minimized and any social life which does not include him will have to go. Her depressions will be tolerated as long as he is not made to feel that they are directly attributable to him.

The financial side of life could be their one point of agreement, both need financial security, but this could be taken rather too far in this relationship. Each is inclined to let personal appearance slide, and they should fight against apathetic behavior in this direction.

Sexually, Mr. Scorpio is the more active of the two, and he may believe the worst when she protests or says she is tired. The insecurity he always suffers from so easily may lead him to believe that she has someone else. If his fears are justified, she cannot expect forgiveness from this man.

An unwise relationship with many reasons for discord.

Capricorn Woman with Saggitarius Man

There may be times when their home will not seem large enough to accommodate both of these characters. He is restless and loves to roam around, and if determined to have him she will have to accept this, or she might as well leave straightaway. This man's life is constantly changing, and his tendency to gamble will provide many a reason for argument. The Capricorn woman hates risk in any shape or form, it depresses her and can make an otherwise stable woman neurotic. Possessing a strong personality, she is quite able to oppose him in this, even though he will probably disregard any attempts to change him. In order to keep such a man she will have to keep a loose rein on his freedom, for any hint of jealousy or possessiveness can send him straight to another woman's bed. Finances could produce further friction because he tends to throw his money around when he is feeling affluent while her first thought is to put some away for the future.

The Sagittarian has a large sexual appetite and, because he is an expert lover, he could well increase Ms. Capricorn's need for sex. But there is every likelihood that he will still sleep with other women from time to time. If she can possibly make herself look on this realistically she will save herself a lot of suffering.

A relationship which blows hot one day and cold the next.

ARE YOU A TYPICAL CAPRICORN MAN?

Answer the questions given below using Yes, No or Sometimes, then turn to page 309 for your answer.

1. Are you a pessimist?

2. Would it be difficult for you to function properly without your career?

3. Is deep depression part of your personality?

4. Are you a snob?

5. Does your sexual appetite go to extremes?

6. Do you hide money in strange places?

7. Does the feminine touch around the home irritate you?

8. Are you attracted to older women?

9. Are you basically straightforward in your sexual desires?

10. Do you automatically flirt when an attractive girl enters the room?

11. Are you accused of meanness?

12. Does the thought of paying for sex offend you?

13. Do you take off for periods of time on your own?

14. Do you think success will come late in life for you?

15. Are you interested in history in any shape or form?

16. Do you have the aptitude for study?

17. Do you think that you were a late starter in sex?

18. Do you need to be at least fond of a woman before you can sleep with her?

19. Is your taste in clothes plain and simple?

20. Do you sometimes feel that your life is restricted by some inexplicable force?

Total up your score allowing three for Yes, two for No and one for Sometimes, then turn to page 309.

ARE YOU A TYPICAL CAPRICORN WOMAN?

Answer honestly the questions given below, using Yes, No or Sometimes, then turn to page 310 for your answer.

1. Do you experience depression that can last for days?

2. Are you a small eater?

3. Do women who spend hours in front of the mirror irritate you?

4. Do you save secretly?

5. Do you like to be subjugated in sex?

6. Do you think that you were born into the wrong time?

7. Do you think that you were a late starter sex-wise?

8. Do you spend much time on your own?

9. Does study come easily to you?

10. Does tradition and history interest you?

11. Do you tackle things slowly but carefully?

12. Does the future of the world worry you?

13. Has your father influenced you strongly, for good or evil?

14. Will you make a strict mother?

15. Are you attracted to older men?

16. Do you think you would break it off quickly if you discovered that a boy-friend was married?

17. Rightly or wrongly do you prefer to go your own way no matter what?

18. Do you take your sexual affairs seriously?

19. Are you a snob?

20. Do you feel restricted by some influence you cannot explain?

Total up your score allowing three for Yes, two for Sometimes and one for No, then turn to page 310.

AQUARIUS

THE WATER-BEARER

**The Sign of the Truth-Seeker
or Scientist**

January 21st to February 19th

THE THIRD AIR SIGN: *Honest, probing, amiable, humane, popular, broad-minded, kind, detached*

RULER: *Uranus*   GEMS: *Sapphire, opal*

COLOR: *Electric blue*   METAL: *Uranium*

Characteristics of the Higher Male

The Aquarian man's greatest gift is his breadth of vision, closely followed by an unbiased and open mind free from superstition or prejudice of any kind. Authority will leave him unmoved and when faced with this he will regard it with serenity or a degree of friendliness and interest, but no amount of courtesy extended can prevent him from turning the spotlight of truth onto the body concerned.

This subject is eager to learn from his fellow man, for the only thing of which he is certain is that he has a great deal to learn about the world, and he is only too happy to withdraw previously advocated ideas when coming to realize that they are at fault.

Such a character can look at life from the outside rather than from the center, and is rarely able to place trust in others until he has scrutinized, studied and probed them, dissecting their reasons for thought or action. He is unlikely to approve should he discover that his own methods have been turned upon himself, however, and will grow restless and uncomfortable when in this position.

This type's emotions are far-reaching and widespread, his feeling for mankind humane and kindly, and it is said that the Aquarian is the hope of man. Friendship for him is founded on understanding and personal esteem, and his affections are well worth having as this is the most sincere of men. He can be lonely on occasions, for it is difficult for him to settle down to a steady relationship of any description, and where memory is deficient loyalty can hardly expect to flourish. Time is given unsparingly to revealing the truth and to telling it; obviously this tendency can lead to embarrassing situations and he may become notorious for his faux pas. The roots of his relationships will spring from friendship, for he chooses a chum as well as a lover, the one being inadequate without the other, and a woman free from pettiness will be the female to attract him.

Usually a close bond can be found between Aquarian man and his children, they will quickly realize that anything can happen around their father: odd people come and go, strange interests capture his imagination, and he cares deeply for his fellow creatures. His wife will need to keep up with all of his ideas, and she is expected to show a keen interest in everything he tackles. Although this type can be remiss on sentimental or important occasions, he tries hard to compensate for this in a hundred and one ways.

He is unlikely to pick a female with a keen sexual appetite for he believes that sex should only occupy a part of one's life and not dominate it.

Characteristics of the Higher Female

This woman is attractive to the opposite sex, they like the way she can point out their assets although they are not so delighted when she also ferrets out their weaknesses and suggests a way for them to improve themselves. Any jealous man who attempts to restrain her interests or contacts is in for a shock, for he will be dismissed as soon as these tendencies come to the surface. Ms. Aquarius rarely rushes into marriage, and if a youthful engagement is entered into she may keep the unfortunate man waiting for years before she will enter into the final commitment. Often others may decide that she is cold for she tends to listen to, analyze and then try to reform her man, rarely being carried away by emotion. This is an attractive female physically, but many will be disillusioned by her cool façade and go on their way. Later she could suddenly realize that all of her friends are settled and wonder why she is not. In order to find her own happiness, she should look for a man with a similar outlook to her own and try to refrain from rearranging every male she meets, despite the fact that she is probably right.

Characteristics of the Lower Type

The wonderful broad mind of the Aquarian is distorted here by growing too wide, creating inefficiency; practical considerations are lost in haziness, and though this character will know that there are many things he could do, deciding where and when to start is something he seems incapable of doing. Opportunities are lost by wavering and time is wasted over trifles. Difficulties are blundered into through lack of tact or consideration and the power of concentration is almost non-existent. The lower Aquarian can often be accused of cowardice.

Physical Characteristics

The Aquarian usually has clear-cut features and a noble profile, often the male has a distinctly feminine shape while the female may have a boyish frame. A drooping head is common to this sign giving the appearance of deep thought. The voice is gentle, the movements leisurely as are the thoughts, and laughter is unusual for a winning smile is more characteristic.

This sign rules the blood; sluggish circulation manifests itself with cold hands and feet. Any impurity is likely to be in this area and should be watched for in order to avoid more serious trouble. Fresh air seems to be congenial to this type when under par.

AQUARIUS MALE

	Sex	Love	Marriage	Business	Friends (opposite sex)	Friends (same sex)
ARIES				•		•
TAURUS						
GEMINI		•		•		•
CANCER	•	•		•	•	
LEO						
VIRGO	•					•
LIBRA		•	•	•		•
SCORPIO	•				•	
SAGITTARIUS				•		
CAPRICORN						
AQUARIUS	•			•		•
PISCES						

AQUARIUS FEMALE

	Sex	Love	Marriage	Business	Friends (opposite sex)	Friends (same sex)
ARIES						
TAURUS						
GEMINI		•	•	•	•	•
CANCER	•				•	
LEO					•	
VIRGO						•
LIBRA		•	•	•		•
SCORPIO	•			•		
SAGITTARIUS					•	
CAPRICORN						
AQUARIUS	•			•		•
PISCES						

AQUARIUS MAN tends to have a feminine shape with long arms; clean-cut features with wide-apart eyes, a thin upper lip and small ears; often prematurely gray hair.

AQUARIUS WOMAN tends to have a slim, boyish figure with a small bust and good legs; an open face with wide-apart eyes, and a pleasant mouth.

THE AQUARIUS PARTNERSHIPS

Aquarius Woman with Aquarius Man

Mental compatibility could be the reason for attraction in this case, friends and their problems will be brought home and shared and each will be constantly involved in one kind of reform or another. Their detached façade may lead others to believe there is a lack of warmth, but it may be possible for them to drop their images at least with each other. An Aquarian relationship will grow and develop and both should find this satisfying. She is capable of changing her direction or train of thought just as quickly as he, and life will be a challenge as they will be constantly attempting to keep up with each other. Monetary affairs may undermine their relationship unless one of them is able to take a more realistic view, however, as generally the Aquarian feels it beneath him or her to give this side of life much attention. As the Aquarian female is unlikely to be satisfied with a purely domestic role, her career will be all-important to her. This is fine with Mr. Aquarius for he does not suffer from feelings of inferiority, and she can rely on his support.

It seems unlikely that sex will play a major role in their partnership for their interest can easily be charmed away from the bedroom, and so even if unsuited physically it may either not be discovered at all or not be considered sufficient reason for a serious rift. In general, however, a certain chemistry will exist between them and such trouble may not arise.

A good union.

Aquarius Woman with Pisces Man

Mr. Pisces may admire the Aquarian woman's constant involvement in the affairs of others, without realizing that her emotions usually remain aloof from these matters. When he is involved in similar situations, his sensitive feelings easily become entangled in the problem at hand. In certain moods he likes to be mothered and in certain moods she will love to take care of him. It may, however, be difficult for these moods to meet and satisfy each other, especially when he is desperate for some warmth and understanding, when he may feel she is cold and heartless.

The Piscean man is a complex character who usually likes his woman to place him at the center of her existence. This is most difficult for this independent woman to understand, she needs to develop her own individuality and cannot fulfill this need if expected to think only of him. He is an emotional man who can suffer from short but deep bouts of depression, and her impatience with this will soon become obvious to him, and when he realizes that she cannot fulfill his emotional needs he may cut her off completely while meditating on which direction he should take next. Her unconventional ideas may shock him, and she could find herself suffering from loneliness. Money is an aspect of life which both characters prefer to ignore, but as the Aquarian normally possesses more common sense it may be up to her to take on the responsibility.

Her physical needs are not as strong as those of Mr. Pisces, and her cool exterior could make him feel uncomfortable and inadequate. She should attempt to appear more feminine and warm in his eyes, and he should attempt to tone down his romantic, sentimental instincts. If she must discuss something when he feels like sex, then maybe he should persuade her to elaborate on this in bed, as it is easier to silence her there.

A difficult relationship.

Aquarius Woman with Aries Man

The first contact these two make could be in a debate of some kind, for he may be drawn to her ability to give as good as she gets. The movement around her could attract him strongly as activity can be a magnet to the Arietian man. On closer acquaintance he will notice that her involvement concerns the interests of others where his own is mainly stimulated by self-interest. This selfishness of his could be the basis of many of their arguments, and when she attacks his ego he will turn the full force of his fiery temper onto her. Most Aquarians base their relationships on friendship, but the Arietian has no time for this—to him a woman is a woman and friendship can only be developed with members of his own sex. He will object when she insists on following her own career for he jealously guards his role as leader and protector in a relationship. This may be aggravated by his possessive streak which makes him reluctant to allow her to be happily involved in anything which does not concern him. Normally an impractical man, he will realize that unless he takes control of their finances monetary affairs are likely to be chaotic.

Together, Ms. Aquarius and Mr. Aries may not be as passionate as either would be with another partner, for each will be so fully occupied with time-consuming interests outside the bedroom that their lovemaking could well be rushed or absentmindedly performed. But this will not worry either partner unduly.

An active but shaky relationship.

Aquarius Woman with Taurus Man

Mr. Taurus' priorities are placed in a totally different order from those of Ms. Aquarius. He enjoys home life, a secure position and the respect of friends. She is indifferent to all this and believes that other people are her chief concern. While he sits in comfort at home watching the Saturday afternoon sport on the television, she could well be out throwing a brick through the American Embassy windows. And it is likely that while out demonstrating she will meet a man who can share in her reformist ideas, thus arousing the strong Taurean jealousy. This man believes that his woman should sit at home catering for his needs and he is unlikely to be attracted to a woman with an intelligent and active mind of her own in the first place. She will feel the urge to tell him that his friends are stodgy and boring, and should fight against it.

Financially, she may have to put up with constant nagging from her Taurean man as security is important to him and her uninterested manner will worry him. Although this relationship will bring many problems, if she can learn to cook and keep him well-fed she may have found the key which enables her to get away with murder.

He is more likely to be strongly attracted to her physically, arousing his over-active sexual appetite, and while her interest is captured by outside events she could unintentionally leave him very frustrated. If matters do not improve, he will start looking for a more demanding lover, and she could be so engrossed in her own life as not to notice until it is too late.

In general, the odds against this relationship being a success are very high.

Aquarius Woman with Gemini Man

Mr. Gemini's versatility and need to communicate could strongly attract Ms. Aquarius and it may only be a short time before she is deeply involved with him. He loves to debate and will discuss any subject she cares to mention. They could become totally absorbed in each other's interests, appreciating the fact that this stimulates their minds and fulfills their need to learn and expand. They will have a lot of fun together whether their relationship lasts for six weeks or ends in marriage.

Mr. Gemini knows a little about everything but is unlikely to have specialized in any field; this can make work a problem and he may get through many jobs in one year. The Aquarian also has tendencies towards this although her reasons for job-changing are probably due to insufficient scope. This of course can lead to money problems, he may provide for a short time then expect them to switch roles. It may be up to Ms. Aquarius to decide how what money they have is to be spent, for where money is concerned Mr. Gemini is a non-starter. He needs some stability in his background and she should be able to provide this without making him feel restricted.

The sexual attraction between them is likely to be intense, and he will be able to take this cool female and fill her with burning passion as he can fulfill her need for mental stimulation. There is little fear of routine spoiling their sex life as Mr. Gemini can be very impulsive and will seldom wait for nightfall.

A stimulating relationship.

Aquarius Woman with Cancer Man

This relationship could start at work, where he will notice and appreciate her efficiency and involvement. But the Cancer man's home is an important part of his life and he expects his woman to spend much time in it—

she is sure to meet with his disapproval when she whisks around her housework at breakneck speed and prepares the dinner in five minutes flat in order to rush out to a meeting or party. He is a kind and generous man who at first will not be perturbed by her involvement outside, but gradually his possessiveness will demand that she spend more time with him. He may suggest that if she must improve the world she should start on their home. Ms. Aquarius will not be amused.

Finances may introduce further tension for Cancer is a sign of shrewdness while Aquarian subjects rarely spend much time thinking about money. Even interests within the home may differ, as he is more likely to concentrate on the past, wanting beautiful antiques, while she can only look forward.

Sex can do little to help the situation for he is sensitive, with deep feelings, and she may consider him too intense. He may be deeply hurt if he tries to be romantic because this can provoke nothing but amusement in her, and being laughed at does not make for a satisfactory sex life.

An unwise partnership in which he is likely to be hurt.

Aquarius Woman with Leo Man

Ms. Aquarius may find this man's knack of making her feel important irresistible, while her absorption in life will attract him. His confidence and drive, both of which allow him to know exactly what he wants in life, will strongly appeal to her, but his fierce pride and love of material things will give her many a cause for complaint. The Leo is a passionate man and her detachment on occasions can hurt, and his pride will make it difficult for him to discover the reason for her coolness. He will always show an interest in her career, so long as it does not impinge on his own—he must always be made to feel that he is the most important thing in her life. If she fails him here his warmth and affection will be replaced by arrogant and overbearing behavior. Although it is difficult for the Aquarian to take an interest in financial affairs, in this instance she may have to cultivate a responsible attitude as the Leo enjoys all the trappings of success even when he cannot afford them.

He is capable of awakening her innermost sexual desires, but at times she may find it a strain trying to keep up with an appetite that far surpasses her own, and will avoid his caresses in an effort to give herself time to breathe, giving a lethal blow to his ego. The admiration and praise this man needs are especially apparent in sexual matters, and woe betide her if she criticizes him in bed.

A stormy relationship.

Aquarius Woman with Virgo Man

Ms. Aquarius respects a man with a quick, intelligent brain, and their love of communication could be the main factor in bringing them together. While she is trying to help and reform the world, he will be trying to help and reform her; after a while she could lose her sense of humor over this, and his critical eye could be the biggest thing she dislikes about him. This will be especially true in the home, for where she will believe their flat to be clean and tidy he will exclaim over its dire need for attention. On these occasions he will accuse her of being a slattern and she will call him a fussy old woman. His insistence on her role as housekeeper will irk her as she will have her own career and feel that domestic chores should be shared. Her refusal to budget and count every penny will provoke his temper, and money will be the cause of many arguments.

Intellectual pursuits and an attraction of minds are likely to form the basis of this relationship, rather than a strong physical attraction. Two critics in one bed can make it difficult as they may spend a lot of time analyzing their emotions and desires without doing much about them.

A good friendship, but these two are unlikely to become lovers.

Aquarius Woman with Libra Man

The Aquarian woman can be strongly attracted to Mr. Libra, his energetic search for harmony, his charm and his apparent aptitude for enjoying himself can all make him seem very desirable, while her independence, active mind and need for other people can lead him to try to make her part of his life. The fact that she wants to remain an individual and stay deeply involved in the world around will not worry him, as long as she remains feminine and well-dressed, for Mr. Libra is attracted to elegant women. He will expect their relationship to stay permanently on a romantic level and will contribute much to keep it alive. She will be happy with this as each will still feel it all right to flirt mildly from time to time.

Provided each can hold his own against competition, life will run smoothly enough for them. Both partners' emotions can be superficial at times and with a more sensitive partner this could cause hurt, but the resilience of these two can cope with this. His circle of friends is usually made up of the more sophisticated type of person while she is more inclined to intellectual gatherings, but it is not impossible for each to adapt to the other. Although it is unlike the Aquarian woman to worry over money matters, the Libran's erratic handling of finances could instigate this.

The air subjects' feelings and desires are normally very much on the surface, but together a strong passion may be aroused, stimulated mostly by the mind. Sex is likely to be an impromptu affair, very much influenced by the mood of the moment, with versatility, novelty and experiment all playing an important part. It may be possible for them to bring in a third person without ill-feeling.

A good relationship based on an attraction of minds.

Aquarius Woman with Scorpio Man

Ms. Aquarius may be madly impressed by Mr. Scorpio's strength of character, and curious about his intensity, while her involvement with life and people will intrigue him. Although famous for her adaptability, in this particular case it may be severely tested, for his tendency to be so positive one way or the other, to like or loathe people so completely and for no good reason, can stir her to rebellion and impair her normally clear and objective mind. Jealousy is deeply ingrained in the Scorpio character, he believes it to be a necessary part of love, while her common sense tells her this can only kill all emotion. Because of this her social life can create resentment in him, but the more he threatens and tries to possess her the more she will draw away from him. She will not realize that self-expression is difficult for him and that when being overbearing he basically needs reassurance, and this lack of communication must result in frustration and tension. His need for financial security may lead him to nag her about her indifference to material things. Her career is bound to lead to further friction, for anyone she comes into contact with will be viewed with suspicion by him. He expects to be at the center of her existence.

Sex is important to the Scorpio as it is here that he can really express himself, but the Aquarian's appetite is weaker and she is more detached, and the very intensity that initially attracted her could repel in bed. If a sense of humor can be developed between these two it may help considerably, but as a rule such a combination can only serve to destroy the people concerned.

Aquarius Woman with Sagittarius Man

Ms. Aquarius' detached air may attract a man whose need for freedom is so strong, he can sense that love will not mean possession to her. She on the other hand will be attracted to his love of companionship and adventure. In this relationship each can retain a certain individuality and they will be free to go their own way. Later, however, his love of freedom can seem too much even to her, especially when she notices his remarkable natural ability for attracting the opposite sex, and although this goes against her true nature she may become jealous and possessive. The Sagittarian emotions, while short-lived, are very deep, and her detachment on occasions could be interpreted as coldness by him and could stimulate his urge to find a warmer partner.

A chaotic financial situation seems likely to develop from the Aquarian's lack of interest in material things and the Sagittarian's tendency to gamble without a thought for the future, and this could undermine their relationship. Her need to channel her energy into a career, however, will be given full rein, and he will optimistically encourage anything she tackles and can boost her up when things do not go according to plan.

His sexual appetite is the stronger of the two, and unless she can accept his finding satisfaction outside of their relationship she had better try to develop her own a little. Sooner or later some agreement will have to be reached as to how far they can go without offending each other.

A relationship full of extremes.

Aquarius Woman with Capricorn Man

Ms. Aquarius may be drifting when she meets this man, in which case she will be attracted to his dependability and his responsible attitude towards life, while she will arouse his protective instincts. The first thing she will have to accept with Mr. Capricorn is the importance his career has in his life—she will have to try to be as interested in this as possible and offer her support whenever it is needed. Her encouragement will be particularly needed when he is indulging in one of his black depressions. Impatience shown with these can lead to violent quarrels. Her own career will have to take second place if harmony is to be achieved. She could be irritated by his insistence on living in the past, his sentimentality and romanticism all seem odd to a woman whose own ideas are progressive and modern. Mr. Capricorn is not usually the social type, and when he finds her friends still around at three in the morning he will object strongly. His tendency to save secretly will be encouraged with a woman who has little respect for money, and the more she accuses him of miserliness the more neurotic he will become where money is concerned.

Neither of these two has a particularly voracious appetite for sex, they are too preoccupied with external interests, with the result that sensual pleasures are unlikely to play an important role in their life together. But then, neither of them will mind this very much.

Not a very satisfactory relationship for either party.

ARE YOU A TYPICAL AQUARIAN MAN?

Answer the questions below honestly, using Yes, No, or Sometimes, then turn to page 311 for your answer.

1. Do you expect friendship from your lovers?

2. Do you think you could throw up a job if it offered insufficient scope?

3. Do you really need to believe in the work you do?

4. Can you abstain from sex for more than a week without noticing it?

5. Do you side-step unpleasantness?

6. Would you get up in the middle of the night to help a friend?

7. Are you a positive thinker?

8. Would you chase a woman who seemed uninterested in the hopes of changing her mind?

9. Are you accused of being detached?

10. Do you make friends with people because of their usefulness?

11. Do you think that to worry about money is a waste of energy?

12. Are you stimulated by good conversation?

13. Can you make love to any woman when desperate?

14. Are you impressed by wealth?

15. Do you insist on the truth at all costs?

16. Are you politically minded?

17. Are you accused of being unimaginative in bed?

18. Do you take part in protests of any description?

19. Do you think you could take a girl-friend back if she had been to bed with your closest friend?

20. Are you unpunctual?

Total up your score, allowing three for Yes, two for Sometimes and one for No, then turn to page 311.

ARE YOU A TYPICAL AQUARIAN WOMAN?

Answer the questions given below, using Yes, No or Sometimes, then turn to page 312 for your answer.

1. Does Women's Lib interest you?

2. Can you separate love from sex?

3. Do you prefer good conversation to poor sex even when frustrated?

4. Do you think jealousy is a waste of energy?

5. Are you a truthful person?

6. Does the state of the world concern you?

7. Can you go for long periods without sex?

8. Are you an optimist?

9. Is it hard for you to change your opinions?

10. Can you make love coldly and clinically?

11. Are you an opportunist?

12. Do you find it hard to find a man you really like?

13. Do you feel that your maternal instinct is under-developed?

14. Is it impossible for you to live a purely domestic role without going mad?

15. Does blue suit you?

16. Are your thoughts for the future rather than the past?

17. Does housework get neglected at the first possible excuse?

18. Are you attracted to a man's mind rather than to his body?

19. Are you a secret snob?

20. Are you a positive thinker?

Total up your score allowing three for Yes, two for Sometimes and one for No, then turn to page 312.

PISCES

THE FISH

The Sign of the Poet
or Interpreter

February 20th to March 20th

THE THIRD WATER SIGN: *Kind, retiring, gentle, sensitive, unlucky, often moody, indecisive*

RULER: *Neptune*   GEMS: *Chrysolite, moonstone*

COLOR: *Sea green*   METAL: *Tin*

Characteristics of the Higher Male

The character of this individual is most difficult to define, for there is a tendency to hide the true self which can develop into pretense. His lack of interest in worldly ambition and an uncaring attitude toward rank or power can mean that he is seldom able to succeed in making large amounts of money. Mr. Pisces is inclined to be indifferent about restriction and limitation provided the inner self is left free to feel, dream and grow according to its own nature. He may shrink from rivalry or competition, and is attracted to the sea, music or writing, anything that will allow him to create without pressure. His gift for interpretation can in many cases take him onto the stage, for he can attain great satisfaction by slipping into another guise and interpreting it, maximum pleasure being obtained when executing this characterization in front of an audience. In proportion to the delight taken in such achievements is the measure of despondency after failure, as he is a sensitive man and can suffer considerably when life treats him badly.

This individual's main affliction seems to be one of indecision, his symbol is easily recognized by the two fishes attempting to swim in opposite directions while their tails are tied together, and this signifies the subject's reaction when faced with a decision, for he will move this way and that achieving no positive result. This is a dualistic sign and one can be sure that whatever image is projected is in reality a mere façade hiding the true personality. Such a trait inclines this character to secrecy and is one that most Pisceans will display, frustrating and annoying those close to them. Other people may frequently try to force this man into facing life, but their efforts will be wasted and will only serve to push him further into his secret world where he can dream, plan and think on his own.

This sign endows its subjects with an emotional, receptive, meditative and imitative nature, but although in many ways this is a weak type, Pisceans have a strong inner being plus a heart filled with an inexhaustible love for all living creatures. There is a childlike grace in this man which may continue into advanced age, and he has a keen love of animals.

The Pisces man is always ready for new impressions, which include an attractive female. He believes in fate and is inclined to strange fantasies which many may find beyond reason. He is modest and when things go well it will not occur to him that he may have had something to do with it, but when life looks black he will wait fatalistically for something to turn up. When it does, all will be well, but if it does not then a well-aimed push from a loved one may help the situation. On certain days his wife may receive much attention, frequent phone calls, love letters or surprise presents, then quite suddenly and for no apparent reason he will withdraw into his own world, locking her out. He needs a female who can provide a stable background, give much love, be romantic when he so desires, and one who can fight the temptation to nag him about responsibility, his secret world or lack of ambition.

With children, the finest qualities in him can rise to the surface, and he will be the kind of father to romp with them whenever they want him to, and in time they will come to accept his quieter moods.

Characteristics of the Higher Female

The typical woman of this sign is all-female. She has much loving kindness, is gentle and possesses a strong and vivid imagination. Men are drawn to her, for she is attractive and, they feel sure, quite incapable of looking after herself, with the result that she can arouse the protective instinct in most men. If the truth were only known, it would be discovered that Ms. Pisces is perfectly equipped for coping with even the toughest side of life, but it is unlikely that the male concerned will ever realize this, for she can make it appear that without him she could not possibly manage. This female should find a partner whose imagination is on a par with her own, someone she can spoil, flatter and who believes, as she does, in keeping romance alive. A jealous streak could cause trouble from time to time, but she is rarely ugly when overtaken by such a mood; usually, she can seem so appealing that her husband will end up feeling guilty and hating himself for causing her a moment's suffering.

Her love of vulnerable beings is well-developed, and her home could be a haven for pets and children.

Characteristics of the Lower Type

This person is unable to make a decision or exercise any discrimination in his life, he is the despair of friends who may desperately try to influence him. The main trouble lies in his receptive powers which are generally too susceptible, for he can listen to one person and act on advice given, and then will change direction on receiving fresh advice from another. Because of this, he may drift hopelessly through life.

This type can be prone to strange attractions and antipathies, which he will make no attempt to control, and which can lead to participation in almost any sexual deviation. A desire for his own secret world is often stimulated further in the lower type by an over-indulgence in drink, and a certain degree of bad luck may also follow him around making life even more difficult. Financially he is hopeless: totally unable to budget, always in debt and sparing little or no thought to the discharging of his creditors.

Physical Characteristics

The Piscean will usually have soft skin, hair that is fine and silky, eyes light in color and a pale complexion. Many have dimples instead of wrinkles and often the male of the sign is prone to premature aging. The features are mobile and plastic, full of personality. Extraordinary grace is associated with this subject, and the entire face can come alive when the Piscean is relaxed.

In health this type can be somewhat frail, but if he is well-balanced and his activities are wisely guided, then good health can be enjoyed. The feet are vulnerable and prone to accidents.

PISCES MALE

	Sex	Love	Marriage	Business	Friends (opposite sex)	Friends (same sex)
ARIES	•	•				•
TAURUS	•					•
GEMINI						
CANCER		•	•			•
LEO	•					
VIRGO						
LIBRA					•	•
SCORPIO		•	•	•	•	•
SAGITTARIUS	•					
CAPRICORN						•
AQUARIUS						
PISCES	•	•				•

PISCES FEMALE

	Sex	Love	Marriage	Business	Friends (opposite sex)	Friends (same sex)
ARIES		•	•			•
TAURUS	•				•	
GEMINI					•	
CANCER	•	•	•			•
LEO	•					
VIRGO	•				•	
LIBRA					•	•
SCORPIO		•		•	•	•
SAGITTARIUS	•					
CAPRICORN	•					
AQUARIUS						
PISCES	•	•				•

PISCES MAN tends to have a slim, straight, graceful body; fine, silky hair; a pale face with light, sad eyes and a few dimples; large ears.

PISCES WOMAN tends to have a very feminine shape with a heavy bust and rather thick limbs; soft hair and skin; thick eyebrows and expressive eyes.

THE PISCES PARTNERSHIPS

Pisces Woman with Pisces Man

Two subjects of this sign should each be able to appreciate the sensitivity of the other, but although this may seem to make for harmony it can mean that they will know exactly how to hurt each other with a word or a glance. Mentally, emotionally and physically they could appear so attuned as to make separation impossible, but these mutual characteristics can lead to conflict, for at times each will be trying too hard to please the other and at others the uncommunicative side of their nature will clash and silence will descend between them for weeks at a time. Each may also believe that the other is far too dependent and will wish for a stronger partner. Although both Mr. and Ms. Pisces are free to follow their own careers, it could happen that each becomes so totally involved they forget the existence of the other completely. Making any sort of financial decisions could be impossible, and this could be the final straw, for neither can approach money matters realistically.

The sexual chemistry between them will be strong, and their determination to keep their romance alive together with their active imaginations should result in a swinging sex life. Because of this their whole relationship may well be based on physical attraction and will consequently be short-lived. Should either of them sleep with anyone else, their break-up will not be far away.

A dramatic but unsteady relationship.

Pisces Woman with Aries Man

Although Ms. Pisces may be overwhelmed by Mr. Aries' impulsive declarations of love, her intuition will tell her that her own identity would be threatened in this relationship, while he is attracted to her femininity and adaptable character which he is sure can be made to fit into his own way of life. He will never understand her strange, changeable moods, but this will not worry him as he does not attach much importance to them. This patronizing attitude may get on her nerves. It may be possible for them to adapt to each other in time, but understanding will never be fully reached. Mr. Aries may change his job many times and each new venture will be entered into enthusiastically and whole-heartedly, and no matter how much this may depress her he will expect her support, which may prove a bit of a strain for her. Her own career is unlikely to rate any attention from him and if ambitious she should find a less aggressive partner. He should never delude himself into thinking that she can take financial responsibility for she may suffer physically under the pressure of decisions; he must be prepared to handle these matters.

Sexual misunderstanding may arise over the romantic illusions she will prefer to keep intact, but his radiating warmth may diminish the importance of this. He will need to remember to be a little more gentle and tender with this woman, his selfish desires will have to be controlled or she may easily lose interest.

A relationship which can only succeed with give and take.

Pisces Woman with Taurus Man

The mutual need for a steadying influence in the background may account for the initial attraction in this instance. Her femininity and love of fussing over her man meet with his approval, but he may not realize that underneath this there remains a strong desire to be an individual. Her more romantic frames of mind will unavoidably clash with his realism, and although he has a streak of sentimentality it is not so strong as hers. Her tendency to become involved in the problems of others may create difficulty, especially where money is concerned, for she is prone to giving financial aid to anyone who earns her sympathy; his common sense and fear of financial dependency are strong features of his personality and motivate many of his actions in life.

The Taurean jealousy and stubbornness may be aroused when her career appears to infringe on their personal life, and his masculinity may be offended when she tries to be independent. When the atmosphere becomes too tense for her she may try to escape into her own secret world, cutting him off, and where a more sensitive and adaptable character could coax her out the Taurean, with his usual lack of tact, will attempt to bully her out of such a mood.

Similar problems will arise in their sex life, for often when she longs for a romantic evening and a loving approach he will overpower her with his earthy passion, and after a time this may develop into serious trouble for her sensitivity will lead her love to cool. Her biggest problem then will be getting rid of him, for Mr. Taurus stubbornly resists emotional change and clings on hoping for a miracle.

A relationship only for those with masochistic tendencies.

Pisces Woman with Gemini Man

Both of these characters possess a grasshopper-like mind, which may provide the basic attraction, but when Ms. Pisces comes to understand that Mr. Gemini needs to exercise his mental abilities on the opposite sex her jealousy will create much friction. Possessiveness is a characteristic the Geminian will rebel against as to him it is not associated with love; he may willingly be faithful to her but pressure can only result in the reverse. Both characters are moody and changeable, and this can make their relationship exhausting and complex. Each partner will prefer to remain an individual and run their own separate careers, and although she may be interested in his Mr. Gemini is often too tied up with his own interests to worry about another person. Finances could provide the breaking point as it is unrealistic to suppose that either party can assume responsibility in this direction; debt collectors will make many an intrusion into their private life.

Her active imagination will provide the mental stimulation he needs to turn him on to sex and this may lead them to rely on solving their problems in bed, but eventually they must get up and face the day, and other pressures threaten to overpower their sexual compatibility. This relationship could just succeed, although it promises to be a nerve-racking existence for both of them and in general their ability to endure such turmoil will be insufficient.

A great partnership for a short, wild affair, but anything further needs careful consideration.

Pisces Woman with Cancer Man

Depth of feeling, sensitivity and understanding of romance are common to both these characters and could provide a good basis on which to build a close relationship. They both need a happy home life and much time will go into improving its appearance and making it more comfortable. Fantasy may bring them closer together for they will be able to share in each other's hopes and dreams. Each is so concerned about the other's comfort and well-being that they could well place rather too much emphasis on small matters. They may have a tendency to dwell on every tiny hurt inflicted by the other as both have retentive memories.

Although the Cancer man can be successful in life, much depends on the woman behind him. When pushed gently and encouraged with love he can go far, and secretly delights in the role of provider and protector. A very ambitious Piscean should look elsewhere for this man will take up all of her time, leaving little over for furthering her own career. He will not mind her financial irresponsibility as long as this is not taken to extremes, as it makes him feel important to control this side of their life and his natural shrewdness makes it easy for him to do so.

Their sex life should be filled with tender, loving and gentle emotion, and romance is likely to be the great stimulating force rather than more brutal passion. For this couple the chances of success are great.

A good, lasting relationship.

Pisces Woman with Leo Man

In a light-hearted, casual relationship Mr. Leo appears tolerant and understanding, encouraging the less complex sides to her character, but once they start living together she will find that rather too much pressure is applied on her for her liking—he expects constant praise and admiration and this can make him overdemanding of her time and attention. He will appreciate her domestic abilities but will always expect her to remain poised and beautiful when tackling even the most menial of tasks. The Leo man judges the character of others by appearance and if she shows signs of letting herself go he will assume that she does not love him and may be led on to believe that there is another man.

Although he may romanticize his ambitions, this is not taken over into the personal side of life and her dreaming will be condemned by him. His pride makes it difficult for him to admit when he has been wrong but her flexibility will allow her to tolerate this. She may become nervous and feel inadequate if he takes on too many big business deals, and the gambles he takes can positively frighten her. She is usually financially dependent on whatever man she is partnering at the time and the fluctuations in their financial position here may worry her although she is incapable of doing much about it.

Such tension could reflect onto their sexual relationship, for it is unlikely that her need for romance and fantasy will ever be understood, much less satisfied, by Mr. Leo. He can, however, love passionately, deeply and warmly, and she may eventually learn to settle for this, although the process promises to be painful. He will not mean to hurt her, but can, quite easily, by ignoring her own needs and pursuing his own.

A partnership best avoided wherever possible.

Pisces Woman with Virgo Man

This warm and feminine woman could regard the cool Mr. Virgo as a challenge. She finds it hard to accept that anybody could be so analytical and critical without being very vulnerable underneath. When these talents of his are turned onto her, however, she will be deeply hurt and in an attempt to escape his criticism she will become uncommunicative. In time he may realize what a sensitive woman she is and may be able to restrain himself somewhat, but it is unnatural for a Virgo to let other people's faults go unnoticed. His life is well-run, and method and routine are important to him, while she makes no plans and cannot be tied down to tackling anything she does not feel like doing, her whole life being run on the mood of the moment. She may come to believe that he is incapable of loving deeply as it is difficult for him to express his inner feelings. So many problems can make the prospect of another partner appealing to both. Financially, further discord could arise for where she is generous he finds it hard to part with his cash, and her irresponsibility will go against his careful nature.

Much love is needed if any kind of success is to be achieved in this union, and their sex life could well be the deciding factor. But his mind and her emotions are bound to conflict. The tendency to run his life on a stop-watch can be carried over into the bedroom, and his predictable performance on the same day at the same time week after week can contribute to a slow cooling of her ardor. The chances of a third person breaking up this relationship are quite high.

In general friendship could be fun, anything deeper a disaster.

Pisces Woman with Libra Man

Ms. Pisces could be helplessly attracted to this man; his charm and expertise in handling women plus his tendency to turn a relationship into a love story which would do any women's magazine justice will all appeal strongly to her own romantic instincts. Both can become involved in other people's problems and their home will never be free from either some victim of injustice or a friend who is in dire trouble. All this can provide quite a strong basis for any relationship, but problems may come when he is faced with her jealousy. This is a woman who usually prefers to be totally involved with the man of the moment, but he believes the more admirers the better.

He will encourage her to develop her own career and she will be free from the feeling that she must be home at a certain time to look after him. The Libran man sees nothing effeminate in cooking his own food and helping around the home. Financially, life may be difficult as neither is endowed with common sense in this direction, and it will probably fall to him to take reluctant responsibility.

Their sexual appetites will be a good match for each other and they should be able to understand and satisfy each other's needs. They both love fantasy and play-acting, and this can lead to elaborate sex games which they will enjoy immensely.

Tension is unavoidable in this union, but as each person here is so ready to work hard at their relationship it could well succeed.

Pisces Woman with Scorpio Man

Although a difficult person to live with, Mr. Scorpio is at his best in this combination for the Piscean woman has most of the characteristics he admires in the opposite sex. His need to feel important is boosted by her dependence and femininity, his jealousy calmed by her eloquent expressions of love, and his need for a steadying influence is satisfied by her domestic impulses. It is difficult to imagine these two not married, for they are ideally suited and the desire for a family is so strong that it is almost inevitable. Her uncanny intuition can always sense his need for love or for a boost to his bruised ego, and although she may wish that he was not quite so fixed and unsociable on occasions, the general compatibility in this relationship will overcome this. Her need for a career is minimized here as she will find looking after her Scorpio a fulltime job. Her financial irresponsibility may irritate him at times, but as this can only serve to increase his feeling of importance it will not worry him too much.

Their sex life should be a constant expression of deep emotion. All kinds of feelings and sensations will be experienced and shared; passion, tenderness, and even lust, are given full rein and their sexual relations will be totally uninhibited. It could be impossible for anyone or anything to come between them.

An excellent relationship.

Pisces Woman with Sagittarius Man

Mr. Sagittarius may be intrigued by the complexity of the Piscean mind, but if he gets too close he may begin to suffer from claustrophobia. He needs room to breathe, to develop, and her continual feminine whims and moods could make him feel restricted and rebellious. Her jealousy could be paramount in this relationship, and the regular emotional scenes he will be greeted with could make the periods of time he stays away become longer and longer as time passes. Ms. Pisces could well, however, sense quite quickly that this is a man who could deeply hurt her, and she may withdraw and renew her search for a more constant man. In her unhappiness with Mr. Sagittarius she may try to anesthetize her feelings with hard work and will thus further her career, but this cannot last for any length of time as her feminine nature demands a steady emotional relationship for full satisfaction. To add to the drama, financial crises are likely to occur regularly. It would be useless to expect either partner to develop a more responsible attitude and money problems will come in plenty.

Their sex life could smooth out many of their problems for Mr. Sagittarius is a thoughtful, understanding and expert lover, one whose pride will demand that he satisfies her every desire. But no matter how compatible the physical aspect may be, outside tension must eventually seep in and cool their passion.

A short, wild affair is more likely than a lengthy relationship.

Pisces Woman with Capricorn Man

Although Ms. Pisces may have serious designs on this man, Mr. Capricorn takes commitment slowly and carefully, sensing and weighing up any impending difficulties. He is basically simple in his mode of living, and he may find the woman's touch in this instance too much; a tendency towards lace, frills and flowers will offend his simple but good taste.

She will have to accept the amount of time and attention he spends on his career, but Ms. Pisces will find it difficult to adapt to the role of second fiddle. She is inclined to make her man the center of her life, and expects the same from him; when this does not happen she will feel ill-used and resentful. Her complex personality seems to escape his attention and his insistence on treating her as just another mindless female will lead to irritation, frustration and depression. The Capricorn's instinct for self-preservation is strong and he is motivated by the financial aspects of life, and he cannot understand or tolerate her lack of decision and scatter-brained tendencies in this direction.

Sexually, his inability to recognize her different moods could bring trouble as with each mood her desires will differ, and when she is feeling sensitive he may assault her with his earthy passion.

Although in time these two could learn to adapt to each other, this can never be an easy relationship.

Pisces Woman with Aquarius Man

Mr. Aquarius is constantly involved in the troubles of the world, and even a stranger's plight can arouse his sympathy, but it will rarely enter his head that he should perhaps channel some of this energy into helping his partner. If this behavior continues for any length of time Ms. Pisces could become bitter and resort to nagging in an attempt to attract his attention. Her intense emotions can make her easily hurt by his detached manner, and she will eventually realize that he does not love as deeply as she does, he expects friendship rather than emotional declarations of love. It could only be a matter of time before one of them leaves. If determined to stay with this man, maybe she should channel some of her sensitivity into an artistic career or interest, for he will never satisfy this part of her personality but he will encourage her in any activity she decides to take up. The Aquarian man is not materialistic, but when he sees her complete lack of responsibility in financial matters his logic will tell him that it is up to him to run this side of their life.

Even when passionate, Mr. Aquarius is predictably gentle, and this will satisfy one side of her complex sexual needs. But she also possesses many other feelings and moods, each requiring a different form of expression, and while sparks may fly outside the bed a roaring fire could develop inside it, consuming both partners and burning their relationship to cinders.

Anything more than a short affair would be ill-advised.

ARE YOU A TYPICAL PISCES MAN?

Answer honestly the questions given below, using Yes, No or Sometimes, then turn to page 313 for your answer.

1. Do you enjoy your pint?

2. Are you secretive?

3. Can you suffer from short but deep depression?

4. Does pornography turn you on?

5. Can you be cowardly when faced with unpleasantness?

6. Is your appetite for food small?

7. Are you unlucky?

8. Does it stimulate you to think that your woman may be thinking of someone else while you are making love to her?

9. Are you a romantic?

10. Are you torn in two directions when needing to make a decision?

11. Do you enjoy the company of your own sex?

12. Can you be violent when under stress?

13. Do you have hypochondriacal traits?

14. Are you fond of animals?

15. Do you prefer to sort out your problems on your own?

16. Do you suffer from bouts of cynicism?

17. Do you believe that marriage is here to stay?

18. Do you think we should all be limited to having two children?

19. Do you enjoy sex when your lover takes the lead?

20. Do you over-indulge in any form of escapism?

Total up your score, allowing three for Yes, two for Sometimes and one for No, then turn to page 313.

ARE YOU A TYPICAL PISCES WOMAN?

Answer honestly the questions given below, using Yes, No or Sometimes, then turn to page 314 for your answer.

1. Are your eyes expressive?

2. Are you a feminine romantic and proud of it?

3. Do men always want to protect you?

4. Are you secretive?

5. Do you retire into your own world to sort out your problems?

6. Are sex and love inseparable to you?

7. Would it upset you if you were incapable of having children?

8. Are you shocked at your thoughts while making love?

9. Do mysteries intrigue you?

10. Do you over-indulge in alcohol?

11. Are you a nervous chatterer?

12. Can you be violent when annoyed or under stress?

13. Does the idea of having a cottage in the country appeal to you?

14. Do you like the feel of fur on your body?

15. Are you jealous?

16. Do you loathe masculine women?

17. Are you easily persuaded into a sexual activity that does not really appeal?

18. Do you change your mind at least half a dozen times before making a decision?

19. Do you need a man before you can function properly emotionally?

20. Is depression a part of your personality?

Total up your score, allowing three for Yes, two for Sometimes and one for No, then turn to page 314.

FERTILITY AND YOUR SIGN

Fertility is relatively easy to ascertain. Two methods are adopted in Astrology, the general and therefore the quickest way is as follows:—

Reducing the twelve signs down to their four basic elements, we are left with three EARTH signs, three WATER signs, three AIR signs and three FIRE signs. When one considers the necessary elements needed to nurture life and growth, earth and water must be recognized as the most important, and using this as a guide the following list is compiled placing the most fertile at the top of this list:—

CANCER (Water)
TAURUS (Earth)
PISCES (Water)
SCORPIO (Water)
CAPRICORN (Earth)
VIRGO (Earth)
SAGITTARIUS (Fire)
LIBRA (Air)
GEMINI (Air)
LEO (Fire)
AQUARIUS (Air)
ARIES (Fire)

The second and more complex method is employed by an astrologer when interpreting a single individual's birth chart (see introduction) and goes far deeper. The astrologer will refer to his subject's chart and make a note of the number of planets in each element. Should the majority of them occupy water or earth signs, then this will be a good indication of fertility, but if in fire or air signs there will be a possibility of sterility and the aspects between planets will need to be consulted. These are the two systems most widely used, very simply outlined here.

CHILDREN AND ASTROLOGY

As explained in the introduction, Astrology endows us with the majority of our characteristics at birth, characteristics given according to our sign and easily recognized in every child.

Aries Child (March 21st to April 20th)

A child of this sign may display many warlike tendencies and, although this can lead to physical violence, he or she will generally prefer to fight verbally. Conflict is inclined to stimulate this subject and arguments among friends will be the rule rather than the exception. Such a child is independent, original, sports-loving and will take an active part in all school activities, with the result that popularity is enjoyed and loneliness rare.

An impulsive streak can be controlled and guided by a wise parent who could, with patience, teach this child to think first and learn from past mistakes, for if left alone this is a lesson that will go unlearned.

HEALTH: An Arietian child is generally a robust and vital one, the weakest physical point would seem to be the head, which may be prone to accident and should always be protected.

THE MOST COMPATIBLE PARENTS: Leo or Sagittarius father. Aries or Pisces mother.

THE MOST INCOMPATIBLE PARENTS: Libra or Scorpio father. Capricorn or Cancer mother.

Taurus Child (April 21st to May 21st)

The Taurean child has a fixed personality and does not mix as freely as the child above, although he or she is seldom lonely, for in general such a character is often occupied in either some artistic pursuit or football, the one sporting activity that seems to attract this type. However, a lazy streak may be observed and it will take patience and careful handling to minimize this, as all Taureans possess a strong, stubborn personality and the parents must endeavor to stimulate the child's interest in some new activity, thus tempting him or her out of lethargic behavior. Bullying should be avoided wherever possible for this can only result in resentment.

HEALTH: This type is usually prone to overweight and can as it were "dig his grave with his fork." Over-indulgence should be discouraged while young, before it has developed into a hard-to-break habit. Throat problems are also associated with this sign.

THE MOST COMPATIBLE PARENTS: Capricorn or Virgo father. Cancer or Taurus mother.

THE MOST INCOMPATIBLE PARENTS: Aries or Leo father. Aquarius or Sagittarius mother.

Gemini Child (May 22nd to June 21st)

Activity is the keynote in this case, for a still or quiet Geminian would be rare. Thought and speech are rapid, curiosity insatiable, and the parents may be driven insane with incessant questions, then irritated when the child seems incapable of sitting still and hearing the answer through to its end. Concentration is poor and he or she will start and drop many things before completion, but this child is usually best left alone to follow its own erratic path, and no matter how many interests are taken up each should be encouraged, as this type is constantly learning and experimenting.

When faced with an order the subject will invariably ask "Why?" and woe betide the parent who replies, "Because I say so." This is totally incomprehensible to the Geminian who forever tests the parents' knowledge and honesty.

HEALTH: Ceaseless activity, excitability and an inability to relax can react on the child's health. It is of the utmost importance that this type should have sufficient sleep and rest, no matter how loud the protestations or how inventive the excuses.

THE MOST COMPATIBLE PARENTS: Aquarius or Leo father. Libra or Gemini mother.

THE MOST INCOMPATIBLE PARENTS: Virgo or Sagittarius father. Scorpio or Pisces mother.

Cancer Child (June 22nd to July 22nd)

This child may have a difficult or hurtful childhood, for sensitivity, gentleness and a fervent imagination can often lead to loneliness. Cruel words at school find a soft target and because of the child's probable over-weight and slowness, this cruelty may be unavoidable. The parents should always be ready with a loving embrace and sympathy but should avoid taking complaints to the headteacher, unless the situation becomes serious, as this can usually be relied upon to worsen the unpleasantness. Affection should be abundant with the Cancer infant, although self-pity and a tendency to play the martyr will need to be discouraged: it may be possible for the parents to teach the child tactfully to laugh at these two weaknesses.

HEALTH: The chest and bronchial tubes are frequently a source of concern to the parents and precautions should be taken against cold or more serious problems may develop.

THE MOST COMPATIBLE PARENTS: Scorpio or Taurus father. Pisces or Cancer mother.

THE MOST INCOMPATIBLE PARENTS: Aries or Sagittarius father. Leo or Libra mother.

Leo Child (July 23rd to August 23rd)

The Leo child is easily recognized, for he or she will normally stand out from the rest of the crowd and is inevitably the leader of the gang rather than a follower. If dethroned at some point, the undaunted subject will break away and form a new gang elsewhere. Full of pride, with arrogant tendencies, it may not appear that such a child is in need of much affection, but underneath the bravado a distinctly loving, kind and affectionate streak can be found that craves response from the parents.

A strong gambling instinct, a love of luxury and ease will all later be very much to the fore of the personality, and so while young the parents must try to instill some financial sense, and make the child realize that nice things cost money and that normally money is obtained by work or initiative.

HEALTH: The Leo is either full of good health or always ill. The stomach can cause trouble from time to time, therefore this part of the body will need extra care.

THE MOST COMPATIBLE PARENTS: Sagittarius or Aries father. Leo or Pisces mother.

THE MOST INCOMPATIBLE PARENTS: Scorpio or Cancer father. Capricorn or Virgo mother.

Virgo Child (August 24th to September 23rd)

Even at a very early age this child's orderly mind may be quite apparent and everything will have its place, chores are classified as all else and put in order of importance. The parents may be proud of such a tidy and organized child but will not be enamored of the critical eye which before too long they will find trained upon them. The Virgo child may seem to have been born with common sense and financial ability but he will need to be shown by parental example how to enjoy life and become more affectionate.

HEALTH: Physically the Virgo subject is wiry and active, and has a large or intense capacity for hard work. This can lead to overstrain and it is necessary to teach the child how to relax and have fun before this reacts onto his or her health.

THE MOST COMPATIBLE PARENTS: Taurus or Capricorn father. Virgo or Libra mother.

THE MOST INCOMPATIBLE PARENTS: Scorpio or Leo father. Gemini or Aquarius mother.

Libra Child (September 24th to October 23rd)

The Libran child is attractive, charming and loving, leading to popularity and a large circle of friends. This is not the sporty type and he or she should not be pushed into sporting activities against his wishes, he would far rather be involved in music, painting or some artistic pursuit. Attraction is felt early for the opposite sex and the Libran will soon learn how to play one admirer against another, including the parents. Attempts should be made to instill some code of loyalty and sincerity, as this subject could all too easily grow up without either.

HEALTH: The kidneys are the physical aspect that could bear extra care to avoid complications in later life, although in general this is a pretty healthy specimen.

THE MOST COMPATIBLE PARENTS: Aquarius or Leo father. Gemini or Libra mother.

THE MOST INCOMPATIBLE PARENTS: Aries or Pisces father. Cancer or Capricorn mother.

Scorpio Child (October 24th to November 22nd)

The Scorpio child may frequently have problems in adapting or accepting the big wide world, for he is fixed by nature or may be disillusioned and even a little cynical when observing his more fickle friends. Any group activity that he or she can be persuaded to join may help the subject, plus much attention and love, for inside the tough exterior is an affectionate and jealous disposition which will need plenty of reassurance. An aggressive front is often adopted when the subject believes, justly or unjustly, that he or she has been neglected, but this front is assumed only in an effort to attract the parents' attention.

HEALTH: Few problems will arise as this is a healthy type, but he will be reluctant to give in to illness and an observant eye is called for in this direction.

THE MOST COMPATIBLE PARENTS: Pisces or Cancer father. Scorpio or Virgo mother.

THE MOST INCOMPATIBLE PARENTS: Leo or Aries father. Capricorn or Sagittarius mother.

Sagittarius Child (November 23rd to December 21st)

A child of Sagittarius is rarely alone and enjoys great popularity, usually due to his or her athletic or sporting ability. All outdoor activities are relished and a kind but firm hand may be called for to get homework finished, for this child prefers to believe that life is all fun and games. Freedom is valued above all else and strict rules or regulations are considered to be only there for the breaking.

Rebellion is common when faced with opposition, with the result that discipline can be difficult to instill, but flattery, persuasion and firmness—in that order— may work wonders where force or aggression will fail miserably.

HEALTH: Apart from the odd broken bone, probably due to the subject's own clumsiness, this child is extremely healthy.

THE MOST COMPATIBLE PARENTS: Aries or Leo father. Sagittarius or Libra mother.

THE MOST INCOMPATIBLE PARENTS: Cancer or Pisces father. Scorpio or Gemini mother.

Capricorn Child (December 22nd to January 20th)

Study comes naturally to this type, for his or her ideas on the future career are formed at a tender age, and the subject begins to strive early working towards the desired goal. This is often a late developer physically and the opposite sex will be shunned until quite late; however, this is normal for such a child and he or she should not be pushed in this direction. Despondency is the chief enemy here, and one that may later get out of control without wise guidance; to patronize or bully could be detrimental but an appeal to common sense may bring the child out of his depression.

HEALTH: Despondency and nerve strain can react onto a sensitive stomach, although health is generally good.

THE MOST COMPATIBLE PARENTS: Taurus or Virgo father. Capricorn or Cancer mother.

THE MOST INCOMPATIBLE PARENTS: Sagittarius or Leo father. Aries or Aquarius mother.

Aquarius Child (January 21st to February 19th)

The chief interests of this child are absorption in experiment and the pursuit of the truth. This should always be borne in mind, for a parent caught with a lie upon his or her lips will lose the respect given unquestioningly up to this point.

Popularity is enjoyed and the sole cause for worry may be the detached and seemingly unaffectionate nature, but this subject loves in his or her own way. Friendship and the sharing of interests are substituted where a kiss or a cuddle is needed by another. It may be possible to teach this child warmth by example, providing this is not overdone.

HEALTH: Blood impurities are usually associated with this sign but otherwise health is good.

THE MOST COMPATIBLE PARENTS: Libra or Gemini father. Aquarius or Pisces mother.

THE MOST INCOMPATIBLE PARENTS: Virgo or Taurus father. Capricorn or Cancer mother.

Pisces Child (February 20th to March 20th)

The Pisces infant is a charming child and one it is too easy to spoil, for he or she is affectionate, loving, kind and somehow helpless, although this type knows instinctively how to get his or her own way. A secretive side is usually part of the personality and there is little the parent can do other than accept this, which is a small price to pay for such a charming child. Obviously, however, a complete lack of discipline would be bad and the parents must try to harden their hearts on some occasions or the Pisces child will naturally assume that it should always have its own way—cute in a child perhaps, but unfortunate in an adult. A reluctance to eat can also be worrying but the subject as a rule has a small appetite and generally manages to survive quite well without great quantities of food.

HEALTH: This subject can be a little fragile but will eventually outgrow this tendency. The feet, however, are prone to accident and infection.

THE MOST COMPATIBLE PARENTS: Scorpio or Aries father. Cancer or Taurus mother.

THE MOST INCOMPATIBLE PARENTS: Virgo or Sagittarius father. Leo or Capricorn mother.

HOW TO GET IN FOR COFFEE
A GUIDE FOR MEN

Surprisingly enough, some girls actually mean coffee—others mean "Come in and persuade me." So here is a guide for the would-be wolf.

Ms. Aries

Ms. Aries enjoys sex and is attracted to the strong, positive type of man, but it is no good being too pushy. She usually leaves no doubt in your mind whether to advance or forget it, and if you go against her wishes your chances will be ruined for good.

Ms. Taurus

This is another positive female who will have reached her decision earlier in the evening. If the answer is "no" she can be immovable, all the argument in the world will not change her mind. But a romantic meal in lush surroundings can do much to increase your chances. Your intentions must be made abundantly clear for she likes to know where she stands.

Ms. Gemini

Ms. Gemini needs a romantic environment, music, good conversation and all the right compliments. Any old line just will not do, she can differentiate between harmless flattery and downright lies. If you fluff the earlier part of the evening, you might just as well go home.

Ms. Cancer

If Ms. Cancer has been recently hurt she will have retired into a shell and it can be tough coaxing her out. You will need to win her trust, but once you have succeeded you could find yourself involved far more deeply than you intended, for she automatically clings to objects of love. This female should be off-limits unless you are prepared for a long and meaningful relationship, so a quick sprint is advised when the coffee invitations go out.

Ms. Leo

Ms. Leo likes the good things in life and may burn a hole in your pocket. She prefers sex in comfortable surroundings, and any man who tries anything in the back of a car is in for a rough time.

Ms. Virgo

When Ms. Virgo says coffee, that is all you can expect. She likes to weigh up her man and find out what makes him tick. If you do not measure up to her ideal, there is little point in hanging around for she cannot be attracted easily and takes her sex seriously.

Ms. Libra

Ms. Libra is in love with the entire male population. She proclaims undying love rather too readily but you need not panic or take this too seriously, instead relax and enjoy all the attention you are getting because it will not last long. Her love of harmony is strong and any display of temper will turn her off completely.

Ms. Scorpio

No wise male will play around with this woman's affections, for should you hurt her at all she will store up bitterness, perhaps for years, and if ever an opportunity for revenge presents itself she will grasp it with both hands. If you really do want to get to know her better, however, you may find that a friendly drink will mellow her and tip the scales in your favor, as a weakness for alcohol is associated with this sign.

Ms. Sagittarius

If Ms. Sagittarius is attracted to you you will have no problems for she enjoys sex and is not hampered by inhibitions. But you must never be seen as a threat to her freedom, she is rarely ready to be tied down and any man with serious ideas must be prepared for a long fight. Coffee and breakfast, however, are easily obtained here.

Ms. Capricorn

Ms. Capricorn will not expect you to be strongly attracted to her, nor will she take it for granted that other dates will follow your first meeting. She needs to be relaxed and you should try to boost her ego a bit. If you can actually raise a smile, morning coffee can be confidently predicted.

Ms. Aquarius

Ms. Aquarius probably belongs to Women's Lib, so flattery will get you nowhere. You will fare much better with an open and honest approach, as long as sex is not taken for granted. If it really is your lucky day, you could be the one who is seduced and dragged off to bed. If asked in at all, it will not be just for coffee.

Ms. Pisces

Your tactics here should be romantic for Ms. Pisces is an incurable dreamer with all the old fashioned ideas. She is all female right down to her fingertips, and will make you feel the need to protect her, although underneath the innocent baby-face lurks a woman strong enough to fend for herself. Once you have fallen in love with her, you will find it hard to forget her: beware any man who values his freedom.

WILL HE WANT MORE THAN COFFEE?
A GUIDE FOR WOMEN

In most cases coffee is the last thing on his mind, but certain signs are easier to handle than others. The list below offers a few clues as to what to expect using Astrology as a guide.

Mr. Aries

Mr. Aries will let you be the guide at first, so if you want him to be good he will play the perfect gentleman. But he is impatient and will soon show signs of worry, fearing that he is losing his touch. He will adopt an arrogant attitude and will intimate that you are missing a unique experience—you may need to control an urge to laugh here. He can be strung along for a while, but he will not tolerate this for long and expecting him to be patient is a waste of time.

Mr. Taurus

Much depends on the kind of evening you have spent with this character. If you have had a good meal and a few drinks your honor will probably remain intact. But sex is second nature to the Taurean man and if you lead him on only to disappoint an uncomfortable situation could arise. If coffee is all you are prepared to offer you should make this quite clear from the beginning.

Mr. Gemini

Mr. Gemini thinks there are two types of women, the nice girls and the others, which is rather hypocritical of him considering his own code of behavior. If in his mind you belong to the former group, the longer he is kept at bay the more respect he will feel. Should he decide, however, to place you in the latter group the word "No" will go unheeded: he knows what he wants and is not above simply taking it.

Mr. Cancer

Just coffee is fine with this man as he has probably placed you on a mental pedestal and will not risk toppling you off. But when refused by a girl who has not yet attained these dizzy heights he is prone to sulking over what he considers unjust treatment, while you will silently vow to yourself never to ask him in again for coffee or anything else.

Mr. Leo

It is more likely to be brandy or champagne than coffee with Mr. Leo—he does things in style. He may consider it perfectly natural and obvious for you to make love, but it is unlikely that he will try to make a one-night stand out of you. When rejected he is a good loser and will good-naturedly accept that he can't win them all.

He could be so gallant about it that you may eventually change your mind.

Mr. Virgo

Friendship comes first with this man, and he is prepared to wait a considerable length of time for anything he thinks is worth waiting for. Self-sacrifice comes naturally to him and therefore ugly scenes are unusual with Mr. Virgo.

Mr. Libra

Any female needs to be on her toes with Mr. Libra for he knows exactly the right things to say and do at any given time. He could sweep you off your feet with his expertise. At the beginning of the evening you may have decided not to get involved, but later these good intentions could crumble in the face of his smooth approach.

Mr. Scorpio

No sensible girl tangles with a Scorpio, he immediately demands to know what his position is. If you attempt to tease or play with him he will walk out never to return. He can, however, generally sense whether his attentions are wanted or not and thus avoid the problems that other men may face, but in any event he will not stay around for a rebuff.

Mr. Sagittarius

You will not get away with just coffee with this individual. If you say "No" he will tease you unmercifully for being old fashioned, and any objections you put forward will be made to look ridiculous—you may end up feeling a complete freak. If he does win you over, however, you will probably be quite happy about it because he is a good, considerate lover.

Mr. Capricorn

If you invite this man in for coffee that is all he will expect, for this is the original Mr. Pessimist. The way to make a deep impression on him is to help him to relax and enjoy your company. Although he tries hard to hide it, Mr. Capricorn is a born romantic, and because of this he is never pushy or objectionable when turned down.

Mr. Aquarius

He may spend all evening discussing your careers, ideas and the state of the world in general, becoming so engrossed that he only realizes with a start that he has made no effort to put you in the right frame of mind for lovemaking. He may then make a quick mental adjustment and rush the overtures, but it is unlikely that he will inspire any form of response. Regardless of the outcome of your decision it will be received with respect, but he may often come away wondering just where he went wrong.

Mr. Pisces

Mr. Pisces is hard to resist, being naturally charming and appealing. If you manage to scrape up enough courage to say "No" his expression and hurt eyes can make you feel you have just denied him the most precious thing in the world. You could finish up feeling guilty, so when thinking of asking Mr. Pisces in for coffee remember that a complex situation is likely to arise.

ARE YOU A TYPICAL ARIETIAN MAN?
(Answers)

1–30

Although you may have some Arietian tendencies they are certainly well hidden. I would suggest that you read some of the other signs for you will probably recognize yourself elsewhere, possibly under Cancer, Scorpio or Pisces.

31–50

This is the score of a higher Arietian: you are lucky enough to have most of the virtues of this sign with few of the vices, and you can disregard the section written about the lower type. You are a strong person, know exactly what you want from life and can obtain it without hurting other people, although perhaps you should focus a little more of your attention on the private side of life.

51–60

You are a true blue Arietian for good and evil. It might be an idea for you to read the section on the lower Arietian several times for all of your faults are written down here in black and white and this may help you to recognize, accept and do something about them. Your strong "me first" attitude could lead eventually to loneliness.

ARE YOU A TYPICAL ARIETIAN WOMAN?
(Answers)

1–30

Your Arietian characteristics are so well hidden they are almost non-existent. Look for yourself under a different sign, possibly one of the air signs—Gemini, Aquarius or Libra.

31–50

This is the score of a higher Arietian. You are fortunate for you have most of the good points associated with this sign and few of the bad. However, a selfish streak should be overcome for it would take some of the tension out of your relationships.

51–60

For better or for worse you are a typical Arietian, pay attention to the section called the lower Arietian as it is written especially for you. If you can learn to control these traits in your character you will be a far more popular girl, but bossy and organizing behavior will spoil many of your relationships.

ARE YOU A TYPICAL TAUREAN MAN?
(Answers)

1–30

Taurus seems to have passed over you pretty quickly leaving little trace of her influence, one or two things may sound like you but it is more likely that you will recognize yourself under a very different sign, possibly one of the fire signs: Leo, Aries or Sagittarius.

31–50

This score belongs to the higher Taurean and you should easily recognize yourself in this section. Fortunately the nastier side of this sign will not apply and popularity and a contented life should be yours.

51–60

You are a true Taurean, good, bad and indifferent. Although you may get what you want from life it is usually at the expense of someone else. Read the section on the lower Taurean, resisting all temptations to dismiss it as rubbish, for it may help you to overcome the more unpleasant aspects of your personality.

ARE YOU A TYPICAL TAUREAN WOMAN?
(Answers)

1–30

There may be a smattering of Taurean in you but hardly enough to really qualify you for this sign, you are far too adaptable and feminine. Search for yourself under one of the more adaptable signs, possibly Pisces, Sagittarius or Aries.

31–50

You are a typical Taurean and your life should be relatively uncomplicated for this is the way you would like it. You may possess one or two of the nastier characteristics described but for the most the section on the higher Taurean will apply.

51–60

The whole of the Taurean chapter should apply to you, including the section on the lower type; try to control your stubborn streak long enough to read this several times as I'm sure you would wish to improve yourself and lead a happier life.

ARE YOU A TYPICAL GEMINIAN MAN?
(Answers)

1–30

You are not a true Geminian for another sign would appear to loom large in your personality; if one could delve into your birthchart it would probably be discovered that an earth sign is your true influence. Search for yourself under Virgo, Taurus or Capricorn before reading any further chapters.

31–50

This is the score of a higher Geminian, you are probably a great success with women and in much demand socially. However, consideration and a little more patience with your slower fellow creatures could be developed.

51–57

If the section on the lower Geminian fits you, as I suspect it does, then you could be the kind of man to cause much trouble for other people by your flighty behavior. You may consider yourself to be quite a man with the ladies, but it's my bet that if you ever looked back over your shoulder you would discover a trail of frustrated women. Try to be more thorough in everything you tackle.

ARE YOU A TYPICAL GEMINIAN WOMAN?
(Answers)

1–30

Gemini has left no visible trace on you, your conservative and practical outlook would seem to indicate the presence of an earth sign in you. Try reading another sign, possibly Taurus, Capricorn or Virgo, but don't try to *make* it fit; when you have discovered your correct sign it will be quite obvious.

31–50

You are a typical higher Geminian, which means that although you may consider yourself to be neurotic in fact you are well-balanced, versatile and adaptable. You could possibly improve yourself if you can conquer your weak concentration and delve a little deeper into those things that come under your wandering eye.

51–60

Jack-of-all trades could be a phrase constantly used when referring to yourself, you are a typical Geminian for good and evil, and although it might help you to read the section on the lower Geminian it is unlikely that you will truly read and digest the information seriously or properly.

ARE YOU A TYPICAL CANCERIAN MAN?
(Answers)

1–30

Your love of personal freedom is far too strong for a Cancer, although you may possess one or two of this sign's characteristics. Such an independent outlook must belong to Gemini, Aquarius, Sagittarius or maybe Libra, try reading these sections for one will be you down to the last detail.

31–50

You are probably an excellent husband or provider and therefore typically Cancer, but some women may be bored by such a domestically inclined man; do try hard to widen your horizons and become more extrovert.

51–60

This score belongs to the lower Cancer. Read this section carefully and attempt to make some changes. Life can be tough for a man with your sign but self-pity is not an attractive asset and it can only do you harm; put morbid thoughts from your mind and keep busy when you feel this mood threatening.

ARE YOU A TYPICAL CANCERIAN WOMAN?
(Answers)

1–30

You are far too independent, resilient and uninhibited to be a true Cancer, no doubt one or two characteristics may sound like you but you seem to be ruled by a far tougher sign. You may find yourself under one of the air signs: Gemini, Libra or Aquarius.

31–50

You have answered your questions as any typical higher Cancerian would. Unfortunately, this sign is a sensitive one and life must seem quite hard for you at times, but a woman as feminine as yourself will find no trouble in attracting a big, strong man to protect her. But do try to be a little more resilient.

51–60

This is the score of the lower Cancerian and belongs to a woman similar to the one above, the main differences are the reactions to disappointments, for this type can develop unhealthy mental attitudes; martyr and persecution complexes are easily assumed and need to be controlled. Read your section carefully and as logically as you can for it may help you to overcome your weaknesses.

ARE YOU A TYPICAL LEO MAN? (Answers)

1–30

Your intuition and powers of perception rule out Leo as your birth sign. It is more likely that you will recognize yourself in the chapters on Pisces, Scorpio or Cancer, read these first before searching elsewhere.

31–50

Apart from some pride and a streak of laziness you are a warm, generous and nice person, a typical higher Leo and so this section will be of particular interest to you. A man with this sign usually goes far in his career and is always the leader rather than the follower.

51–60

You possess many of the good qualities associated with this sign but an overbearing and arrogant attitude can at times lead to trouble, also your tendency to value all from a financial standpoint needs to be controlled. Read the section on the lower Leo and digest the faults listed there.

ARE YOU A TYPICAL LEO WOMAN? (Answers)

1–30

This is not the score of a Leo, your priorities in life are all wrong, although you would be well-advised to cultivate some of this sign's warmth and generosity. I suspect that you will find yourself under Aquarius, Capricorn or possibly Virgo.

31–50

You are a true Leo with all of the warmth, generosity and depth of feeling of this sign. Your weak point will be careless judgement which can lead to many unhappy affairs, try to look a little deeper than the surface and read the section on the higher Leo for this should be you.

51–60

This score belongs to the lower Leo which means the big heart of this sign is mostly interested in its own desires. Your materialistic side should be controlled for this would make life a lot easier for you; try valuing people for their worth as human beings rather than for their bank balances or usefulness. However, not even a bad Leo can be all bad as this is the warmest of signs.

ARE YOU A TYPICAL VIRGO MAN? (Answers)

1–30

Your Virgo characteristics are almost non-existent and so you must look to another sign for yourself. The softer personality you would seem to possess suggests a Pisces, Scorpio or Cancer, so look to these first.

31–50

You are a higher Virgo and so with luck you may have missed out on the more unpleasant aspects of this sign, although the critical eye would still be a part of your personality, which is fine as long as you can keep it under control.

51–60

Yours is the score of a lower Virgo which can have unfortunate effects. You may be almost impossible to please and the way you expect everyone to conform to your strict code of behavior can make you a sore trial to your admirers. Read your section using your critical faculty on yourself: it may help.

ARE YOU A TYPICAL VIRGO WOMAN?
(Answers)

1–30

You are definitely not a typical Virgo, your mind is too broad and versatile. Look for yourself under Sagittarius, Gemini or Libra but don't *try* to fit yourself into these sections.

31–50

You are a true Virgo woman and although you may have many fine qualities it is possible that you may miss out on an awful lot of fun. If you could try to accept people for what they are without making attempts to change them, then life would be much happier for you. Your career is likely to be very important to you.

51–60

This is the score of the lower Virgo and it makes you very difficult to live with, you will lose many friends and lovers if you cannot learn to shut your critical eye on occasions. Read your section carefully and try to accept and then change the points laid out there.

ARE YOU A TYPICAL LIBRAN MAN? (Answers)

1–30

You are far too practical, down-to-earth and conservative to be a true Libran. Try reading the chapters on one of the earth signs—Taurus, Virgo or Capricorn—and if you still cannot easily recognize yourself then Scorpio may be your sign.

31–50

You belong to the higher group of Librans, which is fortunate for you as this is an attractive sign and you are lucky enough to have most of the good points associated with it and few of the faults. The biggest flaw in your personality could be the reluctance you have to hurt others, this may be taken to extremes by you, leading to many complex situations.

51–60

This is the score of the lower Libran and although you may have much of the charm that comes with this sign, you also have more than your fair share of the faults. Read this section carefully for it may help you to recognize and overcome your weaknesses.

ARE YOU A TYPICAL LIBRAN WOMAN?
(Answers)

1–30

Your logical answers couldn't be less Libran. You would seem to possess many of the characteristics associated with one of the earth signs. Read the chapters on Virgo, Taurus or Capricorn, for you should recognize yourself more easily among one of these.

31–50

This is the score of a higher Libran which means you possess most of the virtues of this sign and few of the vices. Indecision could be your greatest fault and one that could bring you much unhappiness if it is not controlled, but apart from this you have an attractive personality and will be very popular.

51–60

Your tendency to over-dramatize your love life and to generally live in a world of fantasy needs to be checked if you are ever to make a success out of partnership. You should try to view your lot through more realistic eyes. Although you are no doubt quite popular, due to a lively personality, you may benefit from reading the section on the lower Libran several times.

ARE YOU A TYPICAL SCORPIO MAN?
(Answers)

1–30

You may possess one or two of the Scorpio tendencies but in general you are too adaptable and independent for this sign. You should recognize yourself easily under Gemini, Libra or Sagittarius.

31–50

Life can be difficult for a fixed Scorpio, but in your case the general characteristics associated with this sign are softened, making you a typical higher Scorpio. Jealousy could be your weak spot and one that will cause you much suffering in life, although this too may soften with maturity.

51–60

This is the score of the lower Scorpio which is not altogether fortunate, for this is never an easy sign to live with. Your critical and suspicious outlook can make you unpopular and if control is not exercised you could finish up a lonely and bitter man. Do try to make allowances for the weaknesses of others—after all, none of us is perfect, and this certainly includes you.

ARE YOU A TYPICAL SCORPIO WOMAN?
(Answers)

1–30

Your character seems to be totally opposed to this sign, I would suggest that you search for yourself under the chapters on Libra, Gemini or Sagittarius for these are the more adaptable signs which should reveal your true self.

31–50

You are the typically imaginative, emotional and jealous higher Scorpio. This is not an easy sign to live with for you can feel more deeply than other signs and when hurt you can become confused and highly strung. Try to develop more resilience to the world without growing cynical.

51–60

If young you are probably a gay and popular girl, the danger in being a lower Scorpio is that you may grow neurotic, bitter and hard with age for the Scorpio carries a sting and one that can be turned upon its owner making her self-destructive. If you can take life a little more lightly then you may avoid this.

ARE YOU A TYPICAL SAGITTARIAN MAN?
(Answers)

1–30

You are much too fixed and sensible to be a true Sagittarian, your outlook on life and moral behavior would seem to fit in more with the steadier signs. You may recognize yourself more readily under Taurus, Aquarius, Leo or Scorpio.

31–50

Sagittarians have the kind of personality that can draw others to them and you are of the higher type, meaning that you possess more of the good points than the bad of this sign. However, a sense of loyalty is still likely to be absent from your mental makeup and this is the weak point you should work at improving.

51–60

This score will belong to the lower Sagittarian, a charming and gay person but one who can be a disaster area as far as other people are concerned. Your insistence on personal freedom and your total lack of financial ability can make it hard for those who come into contact with you. Read the section devoted to you for it may help you to overcome these weaknesses if you can accept them.

ARE YOU A TYPICAL SAGITTARIAN WOMAN?
(Answers)

1–30

Your personality is far deeper than the average Sagittarian's, although one or two characteristics may apply. You may find yourself under Aquarius, Scorpio, Leo or Taurus. Read these chapters but make no attempt to *make* them fit, your sign should be obvious.

31–50

You are a true higher Sagittarian possessing most of the gifts endowed by this sign yet you have somehow avoided the more unpleasant tendencies that generally go hand in hand with the former. Your biggest fault could be one of insecurity and you should do your utmost to put this right.

51–60

Although you are similar to your sister above, you do in fact belong in the lower Sagittarian group for you have many of the faults outlined in this section. Read this and think about it with your usual open mind and it may be possible for you to accept and overcome some of your weaknesses.

ARE YOU A TYPICAL CAPRICORN MAN?
(Answers)

1–30

It just isn't possible for a Capricorn to answer these questions in the way that you have, you are much too extrovert. If you turn to the chapters on Gemini or Sagittarius you may find your true self but don't attempt to make the characteristics fit you, you should be able to recognize yourself easily.

31–50

This is the score of a higher Capricorn which means that you inherit most of the nicer qualities associated with this sign without the more unpleasant characteristics. However, you do tend to be a little serious and reserved—you should try to relax more and enjoy yourself, it would be good for you and for those you love.

51–60

Such a high score could only have been achieved by a lower Capricorn, meaning that the faults associated with this sign will be very much to the fore of your personality. Your melancholic personality can have a very depressing effect on those around you and you should try to control it. Read the section dedicated to you and try to learn something from it.

ARE YOU A TYPICAL CAPRICORN WOMAN?
(Answers)

1–30

You just could not possibly be a Capricorn, your answers are too extrovert and open-minded. You are far more likely to find yourself under Gemini, Sagittarius or possibly Pisces. Read these chapters without trying to make yourself fit into them for your sign should be obvious to you.

31–50

This is the score one would expect a higher Capricorn to make, you are lucky enough to have inherited most of the better qualities associated with this sign without necessarily also possessing the more unpleasant traits. However, you do tend to take life a little too seriously, you and those around you could benefit from more relaxation on your part.

51–60

You are quite obviously a lower Capricorn and you may be a very melancholic personality, one who will usually look on the gloomier side of life. When these moods threaten try to keep busy and forget your problems for you could be a dampening influence on your loved one. Also read the section aimed at you and try to learn something about yourself.

ARE YOU A TYPICAL AQUARIAN MAN?
(Answers)

1–30

This score shows that you are not a true Aquarian, you are too emotional and sensitive. You may find yourself under Pisces, Scorpio or Libra, but don't *try* to make yourself fit, it should be obvious.

31–50

You are a true higher Aquarian which means that the qualities listed here will apply to you, and although you may also have one or two of the more unpleasant traits written about under the Lower Aquarian, in general this section will not apply. Too much cool could be a flaw in your personality, a characteristic which others perhaps describe as coldness.

51–60

This is the score a lower Aquarian can be expected to reach. You have most of the faults associated with this sign but fortunately even a bad Aquarian isn't that awful, although you could learn something about your weaknesses by reading this section carefully.

ARE YOU A TYPICAL AQUARIAN WOMAN?
(Answers)

1–30

You are far too sensitive, home-loving and emotional to be a true Aquarian subject, you are more likely to recognize yourself under Pisces, Scorpio or Taurus. Read these objectively without trying to make them fit, for it should be obvious to you which one you are.

31–50

You are a true reforming higher Aquarian and have more of the virtues than the vices of this sign. You could, however, be accused of detached and in some cases cold behavior, read your section and try to be a bit more human.

51–60

This score will belong to the lower type of Aquarian, which means you have more of the vices than the virtues connected with this sign. Do read this section carefully for it may help you to overcome your weaknesses, although no Aquarian can be all bad.

ARE YOU A TYPICAL PISCES MAN? (Answers)

1–30

Your logical, practical and down to earth answers do not belong to a Piscean. You may find yourself under one of the three earth signs: Virgo, Taurus and Capricorn. Read these without attempting to make them fit, for it should be easy to recognize yourself.

31–50

You have answered your questions as any true Piscean would, fortunately you belong to the higher side of your sign and are therefore not quite so neurotic as the lower type would be, although you can still be too sensitive at times, and need a partner or lover who can understand this side of your character.

51–60

This score should belong to the lower side of this sign, read this section and try to improve on your faults. Your vivid imagination could lead to many kinds of sexual perversion and your hypersensitivity to suffering.

ARE YOU A TYPICAL PISCES WOMAN?
(Answers)

1–30

You possess too much common sense, logic and realism to be a true Piscean, your characteristics would seem to belong to one of the earth signs, Taurus, Virgo and Capricorn. Read these sections without attempting to make them fit you, for you should recognize yourself easily.

31–50

Your score would suggest a typical higher Piscean which means you have most of the virtues, but not necessarily many of the vices associated with this sign. You could, however, be too easily influenced by others which could bring many problems to you.

51–60

This is the score of a lower Piscean which makes you a very sensitive and possibly weak individual. Read the section which applies to you and try to overcome the faults written down there, you are adaptable and could do this if you so desired.